Dreams
with *Horses*

RACHEL M. JESSOP

Editor: Marilyn Schwader
Cover Design: Hannah Jessop
Pictures: Christina Hirst

ISBN: 978-0-9827305-0-8

Library of Congress Control Number: 2010931483

For more information, visit
www.DreamsWithHorses.com

Praise for Dreams With Horses

"It is no surprise to me that Rachel wrote a book which so deeply touches the reader. Many will find their own dreams with horses in this book. The cover of the book alone shows so much the kindness and devotion that our faithful horses give us daily. We have to thank Rachel very much for letting us share with her dream with horses. I wish that all horse lovers will read her book." *Walter Zettl, Olympic Coach, Author*

"Fabulous book, destined to be a classic!" *Liz Mitten Ryan, Author, Facilitator*

"Revealing, thought provoking, encouraging, captivating. A delight for the heart and soul. A playground for the imagination. An inspiration. This book has enriched and expanded my life. Thank you for writing it.". *Lisa Arie, Vista Caballo*

"Dreams With Horses is one of those deceptively simple stories that has the potential to change your life if you listen closely. This should be a required bedtime story for every horse-crazy little girl ... of any age." *Karen Rohlf, Dressage Naturally*

"Dreams with horses is a vehicle to open our mind and hearts to allow us to receive the gifts of life. ... it speaks to the dreamer in all of us." *Kelly Lambrese, RN, BSN, Senior Partner Healthcare Strategies*

"A beautiful read and a gift to anyone seeking an understanding of their own life's process." *Dr. Stephanie Burns*

"I couldn't put this down! Dreams with Horses is a rich, vivid page turner that delves deeply into living the lives we're given. After turning the last page, I knew I was ready to live my life where nothing holds me back." *Terra N. K. Pugh*

This book chronicles it all: The anxiety over change, the vows we make that come from everyday hurts and disappointments, the challenge to overcome our fears, and the discovery of how we can let life's tough times deepen us and transform our hearts. Most of all, it shows the joy we can have in grabbing hold of the possibilities in life with both hands, and living it fully. *Tobi Elliott, Producer, Documentary Filmmaker.*

"If you have ever had a debate with that little voice of limitation in your head, you will love this story. I highly recommend it." *Glenn Stewart, Natural Horsemanship Clinician.*

"I found it truly inspirational. Even though I work in an environment where, technically, we create dreams and make them come true, many of the artists here at Disney experience fears that hold us back. I have already taken some of the lessons you revealed in your book and have shared them with some fellow artists. Anyone who reads this book will learn something to help them move forward with their lives and live their dreams, not just with horses, but with any path their life takes them on. Thank you again, this book is like a golden ticket to my imagination. *Carin-Anne Greco, Disney Storyboard Artist.*

Introduction

Something magical happened when I was 12...I was given a horse. (I had dreamed of having my own horse ever since I watched my first Walt Disney movie where the prince, on a majestic white steed, saved the beautiful princess.) Since then, I have grown and learned together with the horses in my life. Slowly but surely, love once lost from painful experiences in my youth came back into my world. In fact, my journey with horses has allowed me to really open my heart again.

As I grew older, I began to understand my parent's tough decision to part ways and I came to some peace about the whole experience. I moved away from home during my teens and into the world where I began to see colorful opportunities all around. My passion is horses and I have devoted my life to helping people find the same joy in them that I do. The marvelous journey of horses and humans is one I would encourage everyone to embrace.

This book, however, may catch you by surprise. It tells the story of learning to be me again; learning to stand up and take care of myself and to allow other people to share my life. Each story is told with a combination of reality and fantasy, through the eyes of a dreamer, in order to engage the heart and imagination.

I primarily wrote the book for my daughter Shona. I believe she deserves to know her Mum; and in knowing the darkest and brightest moments of my life, I hope she will find herself free to envision the grand sort of life which is hers to receive.

As my life has evolved, I have realized all people need this kind of inspiration, not just horse people. It seems I'm not the only one who struggled, who felt abandoned, or who wished for a different life. At times I felt like an island, like nobody else could understand where I was. Alone. Now I know this is not true. I am surrounded by people just like me - people who have lost love and are learning to love again or want to be loved again. I hope to encourage and invite my readers into a more beautiful future.

The wonder of this book takes you in and out of reality, to an imaginary world and back, from pain to extraordinary joy. Join me on a ride that will challenge your own fears or limitations and also shine a light on your strengths and your bright future. My heartfelt desire is that you, the reader, are inspired to live where nothing holds you back.

**To my inspiration,
Shona Angelina Jessop,
and my incredible husband, Don Carlos Jessop,
who has encouraged me on this quest
to live where nothing holds us back.**

**Thank you to all my friends and family
who continually support me on my path.**

Table of Contents

When You Wish Upon a Star...

The screen of our television was filled with a fairy-tale castle, soaring spires and ornate turrets reflecting in a sparkling moat. Fireworks exploded in the sky above the magical fortress. The anticipation I felt filled me with excitement. What new place would we explore, what new animals would we meet, what new princess would I become as I immersed myself in that place of wonder?

I was five years old and the *Wonderful World of Disney* was about to sweep me away on a carpet of fantasy, a happy-ever-after world where I could share in the adventures of both new and familiar characters, where animals danced, and princes rescued their love, and where everyone was perfect.

As my brother James slept in another room of our house in Howick, New Zealand, I was glued to the story unfolding on the screen. A witch appeared and my heart beat faster. Would the hero and heroine make it? Would they be okay? My breath became shallow and I sat up, unwilling to tear my eyes away for fear it would make it worse. My muscles were tense as the main characters struggled to get through the blocks and mountains that had been set before them. The suspense caused me to move closer, hoping and wishing that all would be wonderful in the end.

At last, they found the key; they made it to the other side. The handsome prince carried the princess off into the sunset and all was well.

I took a deep breath and relaxed my muscles, letting go of the tension that I had been holding waiting for the outcome to be determined. I was so happy and content that they had made it. Ahhh, life was good. It was a happy ending.

With a big smile on my face, I jumped up to tell my Mum all about the cool tale I had watched, and what happened, the great and wonderful and scary parts of the story, and how the prince and princess won the day.

This gift of wonder, of dreaming and imagining, is still at play in my life. This time, it is my own tale I would like to share with you. So, sit back and relax. Come with me as we take a journey into and through another world. Take a deep breath and join me...

Peacemaker

As the full moon descended in the west before the sun made its way into the sky, I walked steadily along a narrow path through a dense forest, moonbeams shining through the tree branches, illuminating the trail with a silvery glow. Even the darkest objects that surrounded me were clearly visible in the orb's bright light. A nip in the air touched my nose, but I felt content in my warm coat. I was enjoying the feeling of anticipation and excitement of a new day as I made my way along the path.

Without warning, the thick forest suddenly ended and I found myself in a wide, grassy meadow. As I looked through the shimmering mist hovering over the open field, something white moved on the other side of the clearing. I blinked to make sure that what I was actually seeing was a herd of stunning white horses. I froze in my tracks and held my breath, excited, but not wanting to scare them away.

They moved with anticipation of the new day, tall and majestic, with big manes and tails flowing and swishing. As I stood on the edge of the meadow, they seemed to feel my presence, and looked toward me. They pranced around a little, snorting their warm breath into the cool morning air, deciding whether they wanted to have anything to do with me.

Eventually, a satiny white stallion moved away from the others and trotted toward me with a soft, elevated stride. My breath stopped as he stood in front of me. His soft, dark eyes seemed to look straight through me into my heart. The angles of his face conveyed wisdom, experience, and strength, while his soft nuzzle made him seem youthful and innocent. A long forelock swirled between his eyes, and his mane swept down from a beautiful arching neck.

His ears pricked forward as if searching for something in the charged energy between us. At once, he both nickered and bowed his head toward me, inviting me to move toward him.

With respect and confidence, I stepped closer, hoping that he would let me touch him, to feel his silky coat, maybe even to allow me to ride him. With anticipation, I reached out my hand to greet him. What happened next was completely unexpected.

"My name is Peacemaker. Welcome to the Meadow of Discovery."

I pulled my hand back and asked myself, *Was that my imagination, or did this horse just talk to me?* He didn't open his mouth and talk like a human, but he was definitely communicating with me. *How did he do that?*

"I can talk directly to your mind," Peacemaker replied to my thoughts.

"You can?" I said out loud, as I jumped with surprise.

"Yes I can," he assured me.

Perplexed at this exchange, I asked, "Why are you here? And more important, why am I here?"

"You asked me to come to meet you here," he stated matter-of-factly.

"I did?" I asked, clearly never remembering asking for a talking horse to come to me. "I don't know who you are."

"Oh you know me well. You talk to me all the time. I am always with you."

Still not understanding what my part in this vision was, I asked, "Why did I ask you to come?"

"You have been searching for a long time now for your higher purpose, your reason for being here."

"That's true."

"Well I am here to show you your purpose."

"Really. That sounds fun," I replied. And then the fearful part of my brain kicked in. "Oh wait, that's scary," I continued as my head and emotions swirled with the idea of what might happen next.

"This is a turning point in your life," Peacemaker explained. "Are you ready to take the ride of a lifetime?" Then, to my amazement, he bowed down on one leg, with the other outstretched, giving me the ability to easily climb aboard.

There was something very familiar and comfortable about this beautiful white horse. I felt drawn to him, and moved forward to climb up on his back. Then my fears kicked in and before I climbed aboard, I blurted out, "The ride of a lifetime? That sounds really great, but where exactly are we going on this ride of a lifetime? And how do I know I'll be safe? And can you see well with just the moonlight? How long will we be, and what are we going to do, exactly? I feel like I know you, but I have never seen you before."

Peacemaker stood up as he replied, "You have asked really good questions, and I understand your fear and concern. I cannot deny that we have an adventure ahead of us. It could take some time. But it is one you have been desperate to take. You have dreamed and wished for an opportunity to discover and reveal your true path.

"I can assure you my night vision is excellent. And you do know me. I have always been with you, just not physically tangible like this," he responded to my questions. "Are you ready?" he asked, and then bowed down again, offering me his back for my adventure.

"Yes I am," I said, with a remarkable feeling of trust and confidence as I moved toward him and carefully climbed up on his big round soft back.

"Great. Let's go."

I grabbed a handful of his silky long mane to stay balanced as he stood up and then walked across the meadow. The swaying motion of his back and the feeling of his feet moving beneath me were delightful.

"Oh my, I am forgetting my manners. My name is Rachel. Nice to meet you, Peacemaker," I introduced myself, hoping I hadn't offended him by not accepting his first warm invitation.

"Nice to meet you in person, Rachel," Peacemaker replied. And then he turned his head and looked to where the sun would soon rise. "Hold on. We are ready to go, and there is no time to lose."

Peacemaker whinnied to his herd as if he was letting them know he was off somewhere. They whinnied back in acknowledgment. Out of the corner of my eye, I noticed a dark movement at the edge of the herd. Since I thought I had seen only white horses when I first spotted them, I had to blink to make sure of what I was seeing.

The moonlight must have been fooling my eyes, I thought to myself, and then didn't give it any more of my attention.

With a toss of his head, Peacemaker began to trot along another beautiful moonlit path through the forest on the other side of the meadow. Clinging to more of his mane for stability, I concentrated on staying on his back as we picked up speed. My hair bounced against my shoulders and the air against my face felt cool in the still morning air.

As we approached a stream, Peacemaker slowed to a gentle walk. The beautiful, clear water reflected the moon that was still hanging in the air, as if not wanting to say goodbye. The sound of water flowing over the rocks reminded me of the tinkling of a wind chime. As he lowered his head to take a drink, I asked, "Where are we going?"

"There is something you will need for this quest," he replied in a knowing way.

"What?" I asked eagerly, never having been one to wait patiently for surprises.

"You will see, soon enough."

The Necklace

Peacemaker picked up his head and walked through the stream to the other side. "We must be on our way." Within moments he had picked up from a walk to a trot, and then broke into a canter. As we moved out of the forest and into a clearing, he called, "Hold on! We have to get there before the sun rises." He began to gallop through a large open field and on up a hillside. I grasped tighter to his mane and leaned forward with his motion.

The wind blowing through my hair and the power of Peacemaker's energy and stride was exhilarating. The distance we covered seemed to extend with every powerful step I felt beneath me.

"Hold on again!" Peacemaker yelled, as he turned left to avoid a ravine. The path filled with stones for a few paces, then turned back to better footing. In the distance, I heard the sound of roaring, even over the heavy breathing of the stallion as he continued to bound up the path.

"Is that a waterfall?" I asked.

"It is," Peacemaker replied as he pulled to a stop in front of a glorious cascade of water.

The power and majesty of nature took my breath away as I watched the volume of water flow over the lip of the stone ridge and then downstream. As I looked closer, I saw a dazzling red light glimmering from behind the falling stream of water that seemed to be drawing me to its radiating pulse. Was it behind the waterfall or was it part of the waterfall?

"What is that?" I asked.

"That is what we have come for," Peacemaker replied.

"Oh?" I replied with surprise, my forehead wrinkling as I wondered why we would want an intangible red light, as stunning as it was, from behind a waterfall. And furthermore, how on earth would you grasp something like that?

"That is more than a red light," Peacemaker commented, reading my mind again. "It is a talisman to help us with your quest. You will understand more about why we need this object soon, but right now, we have a short time to be able to retrieve it. As soon as the sun rises from behind that mountain and its rays touch the waterfall, the glow of this light will fade and you will forever lose your opportunity to get it."

"Get it." His last words reverberated in my mind, and suddenly I realized that I was the one who was going to retrieve it.

"Yes," Peacemaker affirmed my thoughts. "You have to get the light that will help you see all things past, and you have to go now, there are only minutes left." Peacemaker looked in the direction of where the light of the sky was just starting to glow with the sun's rays.

"You know, I'm not so sure about this," I hesitated as my brain engaged a multitude of fearful thoughts. "It is rather cold and I'm not sure how to catch a glowing light, and will I be able to breathe under there, how cold is it, what is on the other side, just a light or are there other things behind there, snakes, snails, slimy things? Will I be safe? No one is coming with me. What if I don't make it in time? Maybe I am fine just the way I am without that thing. What if this object uncovers who I really am and I don't like who that person is? Maybe I should just be happy with where I am."

"Stop!" Peacemaker commanded after listening to my litany of fears. "Your beautiful daughter is two and you need to get this amulet so you can see clearly the gems of your past experiences in order to give back to her and others some of the treasures, learning, and healing you've lived through in your life. Without this I cannot help you on your quest to live your purpose, where nothing holds you back."

His words felt like a splash of cold water in my face. I knew he was right. If I was going to live my life fully, then I had to retrieve that light. Resolutely, I threw off my coat and stepped into the water, taking a huge breath as the cold wet enveloped me. As the strong current pushed against me, I became even more determined, continuing to move forward even as the water level rose to my chest. I was not only doing this for myself, the picture of my little girl was set in my mind, propelling me forward.

My arms were tiring and my lungs breathing heavy through the cold as I reached the waterfall. I hesitated for a moment, but the warm glow seemed to assure me, connecting to my heart and drawing me closer. The light intensified, with its rays penetrating my skin like the touch of loving hands wrapping around me, the sensation warm and trusting. It coaxed me to be my true

self, urging me to open like a present and be vulnerable and unguarded for the world to see. I could almost hear it whisper, "Live where nothing holds you back."

That was enough to dispel my fears and I breathed deeply and closed my eyes as I moved through the waterfall. The water hurled down, hitting my body with volume and intensity. I continued on, despite the pain I felt from the heavy drops stinging my body, determined to reach my goal.

As I felt the force of the water recede, I realized I had made it to the other side, and let out a huge breath of relief. As I emerged behind the wall of water, I suddenly felt warm and dry, despite my just having come through the falling water and still feeling the soft spray behind me.

The brightness of the red light illuminated the small cave I found myself standing in. Moss, ferns, and other foliage were growing on its floor and walls. A musty smell mingled with the freshness of the flowing water, a curious mixture of old and new.

My eyes were quickly drawn back to the heart-shaped glass from which the striking red glow emanated. It was hung magically inside a crystal tube suspended in mid-air. With apprehension, I walked toward it. With every step, its warmth surrounded me and urged me forward, dissolving my fears. I reached up, grasping the tube and bringing it toward me. As I brought it closer, I saw that the heart-shaped object was actually a necklace on a long, black string of leather. I gently pulled it out of the tube, which stayed suspended in the air, and placed the pendant around my neck.

Remembering Peacemaker saying there were only minutes left, I turned to the cascading water and saw that the light of day was rising quickly. I wasn't sure what would happen if I did not get out in time, and I really didn't want to find out. Tucking the necklace under my shirt, I began to move toward the waterfall. Taking another big breath, I closed my eyes, and ran toward the water. When I didn't feel the wetness I was expecting, I opened my eyes. To my surprise, the water had parted, and a dry path back to Peacemaker stood before me.

Peacemaker looked like he had a great big smile on his face. As I reached him, he sighed with relief and said, "Look." As I turned toward where he was gazing, I saw the sun rise above the mountain. My eyes followed its beams of light as they touched the water. At that precise moment the waterfall disappeared before our eyes, leaving rock and rubble on the side of the hill.

"Wow!" I blinked, not believing my eyes. Then the thought hit me. "You mean I would have been trapped in there?"

"Possibly," Peacemaker replied. "But not to worry. You are here safe and sound with the necklace." Shaking my head, I shuddered at the thought. "Jump on," Peacemaker insisted as he bowed down for me. I climbed up on his back and we headed off around the mountain at a steady pace.

As we continued, I could not take my eyes away from the sun's fresh rays shining through a few soft clouds. The sight was beautiful, capping the fantastic fall colors that spread over the hills below us.

I took in a deep breath and smelled the fresh morning air, consumed by the awe of this majestic sight. The trees covered the view like a colorful blanket, the morning light illuminating the red, brown, orange, and yellow colors. *Does it get any better than this?* I thought to myself.

"Not really. Nature is pretty spectacular," Peacemaker replied, catching me off guard. I still wasn't used to my mind being read by a horse. Peacemaker continued, "That is a beautiful necklace you are wearing."

"Thank you. I had to jump into cold water and through a waterfall to get it, nearly being trapped in the rubble and stone if I had not been moments faster," I joked, thankful that I now had the beautiful necklace. I held it close and looked at the smooth, almost glossy love heart and saw that it was made out of solid polished glass. Under the top layer of smooth glass it looked like the necklace had been broken or cracked into many big and small pieces, then carefully put back together. The outer layer of glass seemed to keep it intact. As I studied this detail, I realized that it had stopped glowing and was now a beautiful silvery-white color. "Peacemaker, why has it stopped glowing? Is it alright?"

"It will glow when it is ready to show us something," Peacemaker replied. Content to wait for its message, I looked at the magnificence that was before us and took in another deep breath of the fresh morning air.

"There is one thing that I must let you know," Peacemaker added.

"Okay."

"We must get you back to the woods before dusk tonight."

"So this necklace has a problem with light?"

"I wouldn't call it a problem. Let's just say it would be better for everyone involved if the necklace is back safe and sound before the light completely leaves us."

"Sounds good," I replied. *An easy task*, I thought to myself, even though I felt pins and needles and an uneasy feeling down my spine. "There should be no reason for us to not be able to do that."

Some time passed in quiet reverie, when I heard Peacemaker say in a sing-song voice, "Your necklace is gleaming."

Catching me off guard, I jumped with a start as I looked down and saw the warm red glow emanating out of the necklace. Its beauty drew me in again. I took in a deep, relaxed breath. "Why is it glowing now?"

"I think your necklace is trying to tell you something."

"How does it tell me something?" I asked as I pulled the beautiful necklace over my head to look into it. Before Peacemaker could answer, a panorama unfolded in front of us, as if we were actually part of the scene in real time. The full light of the day shined down on a beautiful grassy clearing.

"Hey that's me as a small child. I remember this," I exclaimed, surprised at the reality of the image.

"So it is," Peacemaker replied as he watched with me.

We were seeing me as a small child, outside on a beautiful summer day, with a gentle, warm breeze in the air. Seeing a dandelion, I bounded toward it, and picking it up, held it close to my chest with my eyes closed while I made a wish. I then brought it in front of my lips, took a deep breath in, and blew with hope, watching with delight all the seeds go floating in the breeze as if they had been touched by fairy dust. I remembered how I had felt at that time, excited to know that my dreams would come true, with the accompanying sense of wonder of when and how. I had no inhibitions, no limits on my abilities or myself; there was nothing holding me back.

Without warning, the scene disappeared and Peacemaker and I were left staring as my necklace

transported us away from the scene back to where we were before. The radiance from the light faded and my heart necklace returned to silvery-white.

The scene had brought tears to my eyes. "I remember that time. I was so free and expectant. It was a beautiful moment in my life. I was just being and enjoying and dreaming and loving and…"

While I thought of the next word to carefully describe the moment, Peacemaker interjected. "Yes, you were your incredibly beautiful, shining self." As I thought back on the scene, I felt peaceful and settled inside.

"Wow, that is something to celebrate." I took a moment to be with that feeling. "I feel like my life is heading back to that place right now. I feel like I am embodying my dream. More important, I am living more and more in that place where nothing is holding me back. In fact, watching my daughter Shona reminds me so much of that space I was in. When we are young we just run free in that place. Now, I do not always flow in my life. I hope that by inviting more of that ease into my life I can help her to keep that."

"You will," Peacemaker assured me, looking with gentleness into my eyes. After a few moments, he turned, and looking back over his shoulder, he spoke again. "Let's go. Our journey is just beginning."

"Just beginning?" I asked in surprise. *The start of this day has been more than enough fun for one day*, I thought to myself.

"Oh, there is plenty more fun to come," he replied as he walked down the hill, deeper into the forest. With the sun's rays yet to reach the section of the trees we were entering, the air felt chilly. The sound of squirrels chattering hung in the cool morning air. I glimpsed them chasing each other, as if in a game of hide and seek. Their furry brown coats and fluffy tails darted from tree to tree, like a series of highways carrying them safely above ground. They moved quickly, darting, and then freezing in place, as if they were playing a game of statues with each other.

The necklace began to illuminate, casting its red glow onto the landscape, and once again I pulled the necklace over my head and gazed into its center. Suddenly, I found myself in a familiar place.

"Oh no!" The surprise caught me as I held my breath, feeling the tightness in my chest overwhelm me and my memories come flooding back.

The picture was so clear. My parents were fighting. The tension and tightness in their bodies renewed the pain in my own that I thought I had buried long ago. Their voices were raised, yelling hurtful things. I saw again the anger and hurt in their eyes. As I watched in disbelief, my breath became shallow and a shadow descended over me as the rest of the scene unfolded. I didn't want to watch that again. I felt as if someone had stabbed a knife into my heart and the sheer force of impact shattered a big chunk out of it. The feeling of despair was overwhelming. Something burned in that spot.

"I just want it to stop!" I yelled as I closed my eyes and wrapped both hands around the necklace, not wanting to watch anymore. "Take me away, Peacemaker," I said angrily, with tears forming in my eyes. The necklace didn't seem to know how much I could handle.

Without saying a word, Peacemaker turned and started to canter through the woods, as if he knew that I

needed to run from the pain and ache in my heart that this scene caused me to feel.

I started to breathe a little more easily. Running away from pain was something that I was used to doing.

Peacemaker slowed down at another clearing. Having regained a little composure, I was still shaken by the picture that stayed clearly in my mind.

"It broke my heart to have my parents fighting, and then even more when they separated. I always hoped that they would get back together, be happy, and that our lives would be like a fairy tale."

"I know," Peacemaker said softly, consoling my pain. As he slowed to a walk, he continued. "It crushed you, didn't it?"

New tears welled up in my eyes and I buried my face in his big thick mane. "I was devastated," I mumbled through his hair. "I wanted the fairy tale life, and I felt like it ended before it hardly began." I paused for a few moments, and then took a deep breath. "It was the first time that I learned to put a wall around my heart for protection. I could never let anything like that ever happen to me again. To be open and vulnerable and then see the ones you love that you hold dear, the closest to you, lash out and do that to each other. It made me feel a deep anguish and the pain freshly re-stirred reminded me of the desolation I felt at that time." Peacemaker waited for me to regain my composure. "You know that I have forgiven my parents. They did the best that they knew how, and I know now that they are both much happier."

"That time is an integral part of your story. And it's important to know that within every hardship is a gift," Peacemaker pointed out.

The Necklace

"Gift?" I said, startled with surprise. I thought for a moment, and then a realization came to me. "Oh, this is where I started to look to the horses!"

"That's right. And what did the horses give you?" he asked.

Without much thought I replied, "Incredible dreams. Freedom. They are my happy place. They show me how to be open and vulnerable and myself. They teach me so many things! They have helped me learn to live where nothing holds me back."

Peacemaker was silent. He let that knowledge sink in for a few minutes. Then he spoke again. "You had a dream come true really young."

I already knew my heart necklace would glow before it did. I looked in the direction of Peacemaker's turned head.

My Dream Pony Zara

"Wow, there's Zara!" I exclaimed.

I saw myself as a young girl with a big smile on my face. I was touching a small pony with soft grey hair, silky to the touch. I remembered smelling the earthy scent of her dark mane that matched her long, beautiful tail. I took it all in as the little horse kept her focus on her eating.

I had dreamed of a horse for years by the grand ole age of 12. Finally, I had my own horse! She had just arrived at our place in Coatesville, New Zealand, walking out of the trailer and instantly interested in eating all the grass she could find.

As I took the lead rope in both hands, I tried to get her to follow me to the top field. She slowly picked up her head, just enough to walk about three steps, and then she put her head down to eat again.

My brow furrowed with assurance and determination, and with both hands on the rope, I pulled on her head again to lead her to the other field. She seemed to feel my energy and picked up her head. We gained a little momentum, walking together as she continued to grab bites of grass along the way. As I waited for my family to make their way up slowly behind me, I allowed Zara to graze.

"Come on," I said under my breath, annoyed at the dilly-dallying of everyone. Nothing goes fast enough when you are in a hurry. "I want to ride," I said aloud as they finally arrived.

I began to relax and gave Zara some pats, reveling in the thought that I finally had my very own horse. My magic moment had arrived. I got a leg up, holding the mane and rope, and flicked my leg over her back with confidence. I had no fear, just a readiness to ride.

Zara did not seem to mind that a young girl was on her back. She was happy to be eating grass. Being up on her back was so comfortable, warm and soft, with a great view. With just a halter and lead, I was ready to move, so I squeezed my legs on her sides and asked her to go forward. Preferring the grass, she did not react. Determined, I kicked her sides, causing her to start walking.

A satisfied smile spread across my face. Feeling the motion beneath me, a gentle rocking back and forth, I wanted more. Squeezing again, I pulled at the lead rope to turn her head as she headed off in a different direction than where I wanted to go. I kicked her sides again, trying to stay on her back as the trot bounced me like a pogo stick. I grabbed a handful of mane to steady myself, kicking a bit harder until we started to canter.

The bliss I felt was seductive. My mind drifted as I thought about all I had imagined it would be and feel like. It was exactly what I was hoping for. This was what it was all about. In the moment, I was enjoying the rhythm of the canter, which made it a lot softer and

easier to sit. I looked out over the green hills, imagining no fences and being able to ride for miles.

Without warning, my body was suddenly flying forward, gravity taking over, and – plonk – I was on the ground, Zara happily eating grass, back bare in the bright sun.

I jumped up quickly, asking myself, *What happened?* I was stunned. My first horse was meant to be taking me off on an adventure, and all she was interested in was the grass? This was not my dream. Where was the unity, connection, like Mr. Ed? She should know what I needed!

Disappointed, I shook off my surprise and got back on, even through my disillusionment. I still had the vision in my mind of how it should be.

I held on a little tighter and steadied my body, this time ready for anything. My determined squeeze had no effect. The kicks followed. Zara responded, moving into a walk, then quickly into another bouncy trot. I tried my best to stay with her rhythm, but it was not in beautiful harmony. But I was happy to be on a horse's back – my very own horse's back. Smiling, I breathed in the fresh scent of spring grass, a warm breeze hitting my body. Perfect.

In a short while, we came back to where my family was standing. It was time to let her eat some grass and settle in. I reluctantly slid off her back and we headed back to the house for lunch.

The picture faded and the glow receded.

"Oh, I loved seeing that again. It was such a magical moment, my first horse, our first day."

Peacemaker looked at me with surprise and a little twinkle in his eye. I knew what he was thinking, responding before he could ask the question.

"Yes, it was devastating at the time for Zara to not know what I wanted and dump me for grass. It really hit me hard, as it was something I imagined that would go perfectly."

"Life is perfect," he responded. "True, just not always the perfect that you imagine."

"I've always had this perfect life expectation in my head, and when things don't measure up, it upsets me," I explained. "So you are saying that I need to accept all things in my life, good *and* bad, as gifts?"

"Everything in life is a gift," Peacemaker responded.

"Zara was a huge gift. We had some amazing times together and had lots of fun. Our partnership just got better and better."

Just then some birds flew overhead. I looked up, reminded of the beauty of birds gliding in the air, seeing the world from an entirely different perspective. Vulnerable, out in the open, they flew with freedom and purpose.

"Let's follow them," Peacemaker suggested. We moved forward at a strong pace, dancing through the trees. My necklace swung back and forth as the luminescent glow caught my eye. I looked ahead as we came to another opening in the forest and saw Storm Eagle, my fabulous Eventer, his beautiful, shiny chestnut coat glistening in the sun.

From Storm Eagle to Sharka

The sweat was dripping off my face in the hot, humid, sunny day. My energy was focused, determined, and calculated. One, two, three strides; jump and quickly away to the next big fence. Storm Eagle was galloping under me. He was so good on his feet, and so athletic.

His chestnut body was covered in salty sweat as we cleared around our cross-country course. There were just a few more fences to go. Our attention was steady as we got a good line. Holding him back a little, my breath was stilted. One, two, three, splash we went in the water after a large fence, steady as we came out of the water. Our energy was high as we ran like the wind together.

Storm Eagle was an excellent partner. His Thoroughbred hooves made a wonderful sound as they galloped across the ground. The tension in the reins was firm as I held all of his energy together; it was a little higher than usual.

Down the big bank he flew with ease. I needed to slow him down for the turn over the car race track that encircled the grass area between us and the last fence on the course, but I was not able to pull him back nearly as much as I needed to. Pulling harder on the reins, I could see the worried expression on the Marshal's face as I came tearing toward the entrance. I was out of control and it took all I had to steer Stormy in the general direction of where we wanted to go.

I took in a deep breath as we touched the track, tensed and prepared in my body for whatever we were to encounter. I could feel Stormy losing his footing in the bark on top of the tarmac. He scrambled beneath me and I saw sparks from the studs on his shoes, designed to give us extra grip on the grass and slippery ground – everywhere else on the course but here. I grasped tighter to stay on, but the motion was too fast. Time seemed to slow down, and I tensed as I fell down by his side.

It seemed a long way down. My hand was not letting go of the reins, in reaction and hope that I could hold on to Stormy and quickly re-mount and head to the last fence. Stormy dragged me about 20 feet, until I was finally able to let go of the reins. He continued running without me.

I jumped up and checked myself. I was fine. More bruised ego than anything else.

I shifted my focus quickly to find Stormy and check that he was okay. Heading in his direction, I was relieved to be picked up by an ATV to catch him. As we drove to where Stormy was, I was suddenly struck by what others must be thinking. My parents were in the grandstand watching my descent where I was meant to jump the final fence. A deep disappointment settled on me.

We caught Stormy, and after quickly checking him out, I saw that he was fine and hadn't hurt himself. My embarrassment quickly turned to frustration, helping me to stay focused. I remounted and we walked, trotted, and

then cantered. My energy was high, and I was nervous from the events that had just happened.

Eventually, we got a nice rhythm. I squeezed my legs extra tight and counted my strides again into the last fence. There was no way I was not going to jump the last fence clear. We sailed through the air and cantered through to the finish flags. Afterward, I walked him around a while to let him settle and cool his muscles down.

The emotion of what had just happened hit me then. I burst into tears and, not wanting to look stupid, tried to look as though I was fine. My hopes and expectations were shattered. I had the ability to win this event, to go clear. Blame set in. Why didn't they put enough bark down?

Then a feeling of helplessness set in, and a lump lodged in my throat. I was no longer able to hold back the tears. What did I do to deserve this? My disappointment was written all over my face.

I took Stormy back to the truck, having to look after his needs, regardless of how I felt. No matter how deep my emotions were, I would not allow them to affect him.

As the picture faded, I could feel a small shaft of pain in my heart. I lifted my hand and gently rubbed the spot. I realized aloud, "Wow, I had a lot on the line, with huge expectations on myself at that time. I wanted to be the best. I guess that hasn't changed."

"Not at all. You also had a whole lot of fun," Peacemaker gently reminded me.

"Yes, I did. There is nothing like going fast with a horse!"

Peacemaker looked at me. "I guess you know all about that, huh?" he chuckled.

From Storm Eagle to Sharka

"Interesting that Stormy did really well considering he was an ex-steeplechaser and he had raced at that venue before. The loud speakers made him think we were at the races from the first day that we got there. He was really charged up."

I thought back to my decision to sell him. I realized how disappointed I was in allowing what other people thought about him – "he is not good enough to take you to the next level" – to influence me to part with him. *That was one of the biggest regrets I had in life,* I thought to myself.

"I had a huge amount of fun with Storm Eagle," I said aloud. "He could have taken me to the next level. I just did not have the skills or know how to move forward. Even so, Stormy and I did extremely well, usually in the top 10. We were a great combination. But I really did get to a point where I did not know how to move both of us to the next level," I sighed.

"There comes a point in everyone's life where you end up moving forward whether you want to or not. It always comes in a different package," Peacemaker observed.

Just then the wind picked up and blew a few leaves into the air. "Look at the leaves," Peacemaker urged as I watched them dance in the breeze, swirling so free and animated, with the ability to go anywhere at any moment with the help of the wind.

Once again, I felt a tug at my heart and looked to see my necklace glowing.

"Sharka," I whispered, smiling at the image that appeared.

That big, 16.2-hand Thoroughbred liver chestnut always put a smile on my face. He had so much power

and talent. I was in awe of him, with his chiseled muscles speaking out his strength. I was drawn to him, and yet afraid of him at the same time. The first time I was asked if I would like to ride him, it struck a chord in my heart.

I had watched him for a while, admiring his talent in jumping. He would canter sideways, his head tucked into his chest with his tongue hanging out, lathered with sweat, high energy bursting from his body. Then, at the last minute, he would straighten his body, take one stride at the base of the jump, then with ease, jump a five-foot high and wide obstacle and clear it with air. I imagined the incredible possibilities this horse had.

I took the reins and put my foot in the stirrup, noticing the long way up on this great big horse. I had to take a firm hold of the saddle to help me climb up. I could feel his energy as I sat in the saddle, almost as if I was a plug and he was the power socket and now we were switched on. Sharka started to walk off, and I allowed him to, feeling the power in his purposeful walk, like he was in a hurry to get somewhere.

We were in an arena about 40 x 30 meters in size, so with confidence, I thought to myself, "Why not trot?" As I thought about this I barely had to touch my legs to his sides and he willingly moved into a trot. While I'm always eager to feel a horse's energy and speed, I found my breathing erratic. There was something I sensed about this horse that made me feel cautious.

As we came around the corner of the arena, Sharka jumped into a canter on his own, which I thought was fine at first. His canter was so strong and powerful and forward, that the feeling carried me away. Then he picked up speed. I shortened the reins, worried about how I would stop this horse that I did not really know well.

I pulled on the reins as Sharka picked up even more speed. I was beginning to feel frightened, and completely out of control. In exasperation, I pulled on the reins again as hard as I could. Apparently, Sharka thought that meant to go faster.

My brain switched to calculating the area and risks. The arena fence was not very big compared to the heights I had seen this horse jump. He could sail over this fence very easily. My body was tense as I kept pulling on the reins. He just kept on pushing and picking up speed.

My adrenaline soared, an unpleasant feeling of despair racing through my body, as I now had no idea what to do. I pulled harder and harder, and then suddenly, without reason, he started to slow.

Not knowing what I did to communicate to him that I wanted him to stop, a rush of relief flooded my body as he began to slow down. I started breathing again, pleased that nothing had happened. However, this horse had taken me to the edge and nearly over in a very short ride. It had left me scared, but strangely excited at the same time.

Still feeling the adrenaline rush as the picture faded, I said to Peacemaker, "I loved that horse. He taught me so much. He frightened me a few times, but he really made me start to search for a better way to communicate with a horse. I'm so thankful for him."

"How did you get him?"

"Amazingly, I got him for free. I was inspired by his potential, and didn't have a horse at the time. No one else wanted him, even with all his talent, because he was so much horse. The owner was talking about pet food, and I

couldn't have that, so I acquired him. He was a hugely talented horse, but it was a little crazy for me to take on so much horse."

"It was the right thing for you at the time," Peacemaker assured me.

"Speaking of time, it is amazing how much time it takes when you have to take the time. It took three or four years at home to get him to a place where he was ready to compete."

"You competed? How was that?"

My necklace beamed red again.

"I bet we are going to see," Peacemaker added, as we looked at the necklace in anticipation.

There I was in Taupo, New Zealand. I had tacked Sharka up and we were heading over for the Show Jumping. He felt fresh, the early spring sun keeping everybody at the show warm. Our energy was high, with horses and their riders waiting their turn, and spectators lingering around us.

It had been a long time since I had been competing, and I was excited to be out again. Our dressage test earlier in the day had made me happy and I was ready for what was coming up next.

I warmed Sharka up by trotting a few circles and popping over a few small fences. As always, he had a huge amount of energy, so I tried to take it slow.

Curious to know how much time we had before our turn, we rode over to the posted schedule and I saw that there were two riders to go before us. We made our way over to the entrance, Sharka's energy rising with every step that took us closer. I guided him where he could see the fences, the colored poles and stands holding them up, the pretty flower pots and numbers marking each fence's jump order. The rope marking the border of the area seemed to have a sign on it shouting, "Keep Out!"

Suddenly, he spun around and reared up, standing on his back legs and waving his front legs around and around like he was riding an imaginary bicycle. I tried turning him, patting him, telling him it was okay. Nothing I said or did encouraged him to go near the arena or calm down.

I searched my mind for something I could do to help him. Although my fear lessened as time passed, I could not think of anything to do differently, and just as soon as I thought he was settling down, he would rear again.

My turn in the show jumping came and went. Determined not to give up, we stayed outside the entrance for two hours. He finally stopped the big rears, but was still beside himself. I dismounted and led him toward the jumping arena. He still did not want to go anywhere near it, whether I was on or off of him. My hope was to at least go there and show him it was okay. However, he would have no part in it.

Disappointment was written all over my face and body as I walked him back to the truck, un-tacked him, and put him away in his pen. He was still filled with energy and continued running around his pen. Struck with doubt, I asked myself, *Can I ever help this talented horse do and be what he is so brilliant at doing?* Disillusioned, I found a quiet spot in my truck and cried at the letdown of the day, my chest tight with frustration and defeat. I was out of ideas and tired. On top of everything, I still had to drive home, a long four-hour trip.

As I sat on Peacemaker, watching the scene unfold again in front of me, I thought aloud, "If there was

anything that could take someone to the edge and make them give up, that would have been the time."

"Yes," Peacemaker agreed, then added, "But what did it really do? Did you give up?"

I sighed, and then replied, "No. I was ready to try anything. I was out of ideas. It took me to rock bottom."

"Anything else?" Peacemaker encouraged.

"Yes. When you reach rock bottom, you can either stay there or realize that the only place to go next is up. I was ready and open to learn and grow. It's amazing what these disasters do for us in our life. If he had been an easy, straightforward horse, I may not have been ready to find another way to communicate with him." I paused for a moment. "What a blessing Sharka was for me. He had a lot to teach me."

"He sure was a blessing," Peacemaker agreed.

I felt a big drop of water hit me and we both looked up as rain began to fall from the sky.

"I think we are going to be in for a little storm. Let's shelter under that big tree over there," Peacemaker suggested as he moved toward the canopy. I slid off his back and crouched under his neck. The tree was huge and gave us great protection as the storm picked up in intensity.

"Peacemaker, my necklace is glowing again." Happy for the distraction from the weather, we both looked at the image it revealed.

Gate of Decision

The lights were turned down low in the big auditorium as I sat with a few friends listening to Dr. Robert Miller present his lecture. He had piqued my curiosity with his concepts on foal imprinting and horse/mule training. I was riveted to my seat as the video came on, excited to see all I could pick up on this new, natural way of working with horses. I was mesmerized as I watched a guy with a cowboy hat riding a white horse. I thought it very cool that he was bareback, staying on, but bridle-less. *What? There is nothing at all on the horse's head?* I thought.

He cantered and then jumped. My mouth nearly hit the floor. He cantered up and down hills, and then did a simple and flying lead change. But the most significant piece for me was when he stopped fast and clean, exactly when his rider wanted him to.

I was flabbergasted. I had never seen anything like it in my life. I couldn't believe that anyone could actually do that. I was also hopeful and excited that maybe I could do it, too.

As the seminar went on, Dr. Miller explained a better way of training and handling horses. I had never heard

of the technique before, but was excited to try these new ideas. I was also devastated that I had been doing some of the things that I had without realizing what I was doing. My friends and I had tears in our eyes at the break. The moment was life changing. And what we had seen was just the start to a day full of amazement.

A lady stood up during the seminar and told us that the man riding the white horse was Pat Parelli, and that he was coming to New Zealand that year. I was excited, and hooked.

"I want to learn how to do that. Let's go!"

"Great idea," Peacemaker agreed.

"Oh!" Caught by surprise, the story had stopped, but I was still in the moment and going with it. "I guess I was pretty excited to see that someone could do things on a horse that I didn't even know were possible."

"I guess you were," Peacemaker agreed, as we both giggled. In our connection to the scene, we hadn't realized that the rain had stopped. "Whew, that was quite a rain storm. Speaking of water, I'm thirsty. Do you know if we are near any water? Horses have a fantastic sense of smell, don't they?"

"Yes we do, and there is water close."

"It's handy having a horse around," I joked.

As we walked through some more trees, we startled some deer, and ourselves in the process. We watched them bound off into the distance, their white tails in the air, running as if their life depended on it, nature in its true form. My necklace diverted our attention as its rays reflected off the scene and we stopped to watch.

My excitement was overflowing as Pat and Linda Parelli came out and introduced themselves, then explained what Natural Horsemanship was all about.

Gate of Decision

The concepts were so new and different that it wasn't easy to get my head around everything that he was explaining. *Seven games. Okay, games with horses. That's different. I just want to stop my horse, but I'm open to games if they help me to achieve that*, I thought to myself as he went on.

We moved outside and started playing with those seven games, moving our horses around. Pat would demonstrate what we were to ask for, with a different horse for each game. He made it look simple and easy, getting every horse that he touched to do what he was asking with seemingly no effort.

I found out very quickly that it was not as easy as it looked. I would try a move and it simply did not go as I expected. I felt like a two-year old trying to get a square shape to fit into the round hole. I pushed harder and harder, as if that would make it work, then felt complete frustration when it didn't happen as I wanted it to.

What made it worse was that I was not two, and I had a big, strong, powerful horse on the end of my line feeding off my energy. He danced away from me when I moved my hands, asking him to go away from the pressure. But he didn't go in the direction I wanted. Following him to just get him to stop seemed to make him move away even more.

Holding on to the last piece of composure I had, with irritation I said under my breath, "What is the point of this game anyway?"

Pat's assistant came over to help. "Slow down a little. Keep your feet still." From the state I was in, his suggestion seemed to be mocking me. "Can I help you?" he continued, shifting his approach from telling to asking.

"Yes, please," I relented, annoyed that I couldn't get the concept, but relieved that I could get help. At the time, I hoped that he would have no luck, too, so I could validate my own failure. Despite that, I hoped he could help me learn this seemingly difficult new way of working with horses.

He took my horse's lead and got in the right position, then using the right amount of energy and direction, he helped Sharka fluidly move sideways and asked him to stop. Thankfully for my sanity, he did not get an immediate stop either. But he did get some soft, quiet steps, and eventually Sharka stopped.

"Thanks," I replied, a little astonished that he was able to achieve that result so easily, and pleased that Sharka could do it without all the dancing around. Then I tried it. Watching someone else do something makes me feel like I can just go and do whatever it is, just like that, and get a perfect result. Although my next effort was better than what I had done previously, it was nowhere near as good as what Pat's assistant was able to do. This fed my frustration.

I was determined, and so tried again. The assistant walked past again later, calling out, "Slow down." I took in a breath to try to slow down. It helped, but my brain was on overwhelm with all the new information, and I was upset with myself that I wasn't getting the results that others were getting more quickly. I wanted to give up. I felt a sharp ache in my heart, as I was conflicted: face the frustration of this new stuff or go back to how it was. Sharka stopped, turned his head, and looked at me, his eyes penetrating my soul. The ache lessened, and with hesitation, I surrendered to the process.

Gate of Decision

This feeling of surrender was new. I had doubted that Sharka and I could ever get this. But the look Sharka gave me... There was something in the back of my mind that kept reminding me of that vision of Pat stopping while riding that white horse with nothing on its head. I had no clue how it would all come together, but I wanted it.

At the lunch break, I was looking through the information laid out on a table and I saw their Levels program. I picked up the sheet and started to read it, my eyes nearly popping out of my head with surprise. *They want us to do what to pass this Level One test?* I thought to myself. I reread some of the list: Riding bareback with just a halter and a 9' string attached; going forward in walk and trot, then stop and back up. As I kept reading, I thought that some of those tasks would be impossible for me to achieve with Sharka, but at the same time, I really wanted to do it. I really wanted to know how. How amazing it would be when and if I could do that.

My attention came back to the forest as Peacemaker and I continued to walk. "I came away from that clinic with my paradigm shifted. I didn't really understand completely how what we did matched what we would be asked to do at Level One, or how it would get to that cool video I had seen at the seminar. But I was going to give it my best shot."

"And how exactly did you go about doing that?" Peacemaker teased.

My necklace started to glow again. "I guess we are about to find out."

The view that came before us was of Sharka and me in the morning before work. I loved being up before sunrise. I would get Sharka ready in the lighted barn, and as daylight began to peek through the windows in

anticipation of the new day, we would start playing. I was determined to get good at this friendly game thing.

We walked out into the field with my Parelli equipment. I picked up my long, stiff carrot stick and started to wave it through the air, then let the 9' string attached to the end of it slap the ground to my left, and then my right. As the rope swung through the air it made a whizzing sound and a great big "swack" as it hit the ground. Sharka, not liking it at all, pulled back at the end of the line. Thankfully it was a Parelli line and much longer than what I would normally have to hold onto. Sharka reared and jumped and started taking me with him. I tried to stay grounded with my feet, but he was so strong he dragged me around. I had to move to stay upright.

I was determined to get him familiar with this friendly game, at the same time my head was saying, *This is not the picture of friendly*. I was frustrated, having more questions than answers. *How do I get him to accept this thing? Why is he so reactive?*

As we continued, the carrot stick and the string felt heavier and heavier. I was focused and determined and we whizzed around for ages. Annoyed with the results I was getting, I wanted to throw the stick and string down and scream and yell, and… "I should just give this stuff up," I said to myself in a muted whisper. "Where are we going with this? What do I do, go forward with this new way, or back to what I know and keep on trying?" That question continued to buzz in my head.

When I looked at it, I was not very successful with what I had been doing. But then, I wasn't very successful with the new stuff either. "This is all too hard," I said to myself, then looked up into Peacemaker's eyes. The scene had ended, but I was still there in the moment.

"There are two options with the gate of change," Peacemaker said as he moved his head toward two enormous gates that appeared out of nowhere. Their size was intimidating and daunting. They appeared to be made out of heavy metal, taller than anything I had ever seen. They were wide with massive, dark stone walls jutting out on both sides of each entrance. I could see nothing to hold onto and nothing to climb. "Stay in this place and take the nice easy path," he gestured to the very inviting, plain path that just led us straight back to where we started. "Or, continue on, make the decision to keep trying, and move forward," he finished as he directed my view through the gates to the other adventurous path, a more difficult, but exciting trek.

I looked at the task, feeling overwhelmed, knowing that I wanted to keep going and somehow open the gates of change, but feeling defeated and not knowing how I was going to do it. Even if I could get to the other side, would I be strong enough to continue on this path of self-revelation? The soft, easy way looked inviting, with its comfortable and familiar look, but I didn't want to go back to where we had started.

Peacemaker interrupted my thoughts. "Where is the adventure in comfortable and familiar? Where is the growth and learning? Where is the passion and excitement? Life is an adventure. It ebbs and flows, with ups and downs. Those things are the interesting things, the things that make life, life."

I knew that what Peacemaker was saying was true. I walked up to the gates to see if I could push them open, but could not even make them budge. Then I noticed a

great big lock on a large chain that was draped around each of them that I had not noticed before. I had been so overwhelmed with their size I had not seen this important detail. "Great," I said in dismay. "Not only are they massive and forbidding, they are locked and I don't have a key."

With disillusionment, I sighed and walked to a big rock, sat down, and put my head in my hands, my elbows resting on my knees. My head was buzzing again. "This is so hard. I'm not sure how to get over, around, or through the gates. Maybe this is all too big for me. Maybe I'm not that thing I had hoped to be. Maybe I am just dreaming to go any farther."

I felt the weight of the burden like a big, wet blanket over me. Even my breathing became shallow and awkward. I had expected my adventure to be easier than this. On my very own fairy tale, I had expected to be an over-comer. But this was all too immense for me. "I'm stuck. I am here and I don't know where to look, or turn to next." A feeling of complete self-pity consumed me. I was too devastated to even cry. I felt the dull ache in my heart again. I wanted it all to go away. Then I just shut down, feeling numb, with no way to move forward.

Peacemaker walked over to where I was sitting, and instead of comforting me, he lowered his head and pushed me off the rock. Surprised, I landed in a heap on the ground. "How many stories will you have if you take the easy road?" he demanded. "You could say, well the easy road was predictable so that's why I took it. But is that what you truly want?"

My first thought was that I could identify with that idea. Moving slowly and steadily is consistent and confidence building. I could be fine by staying exactly the same and feel incredibly in control of my world. If things happened to throw me off course, I could quickly get them under control again and stay with how I was doing things. I wanted that to be what I could imagine for myself. But it just wasn't sitting with me at all. The cold hard reality of the truth slapped me hard. I slowly sat up, ready to listen, even though I wasn't quite ready to get up and try again.

Peacemaker continued. "Or, when you give an account of your life, you could say, 'I ran against obstacles, but worked out how to get over, around, under, or through them, and pushed on, ready for the next challenge. Each challenge made me brighter and wiser, and now I have so much more to share. I feel satisfied and fulfilled. I make decisions. I learn. I still doubt, too, but that's okay.' It's been challenging at times, but really, what is your choice if you want to truly have an amazing relationship with your horse, and if you want to progress and learn to stop this horse without reins?" He paused for a moment, waiting for it all to sink in. "You have no other choice."

Peacemaker was right, I thought to myself. I slowly stood up. My expectation had been that I would just be able to communicate with my horse in a new way and do amazing stuff after one clinic, and that didn't happen.

"How many times did Edison try to make a light bulb?" Peacemaker asked as I touched the big iron gate again, pushing on it to see if it would even move.

"Wasn't it something like 999 times, and it finally worked on the 1000th try?" I replied. "But he knew it was going to happen."

Catching my sarcasm, Peacemaker replied, "Oh, he doubted too. But there was a difference. He just kept on

trying, knowing that there had to be a way. In your case, you even have someone else who has already done it before you."

I moved to the big lock and held it with two hands, looking into the large empty keyhole. *What a weird shape*, I thought to myself. "How come it did not just happen for me if someone else had already done it? And I wasn't even sure I was on the right track," I countered. Realizing the parallel between the scene of the past and my current predicament, I came back to the present. "Is passing through these gates even the way I want to go?"

"How many times did you try?"

"This was my…" I stopped as the recognition of my impatience sunk in "…first big try after the clinic."

I dropped the lock and moved over to the other gate. I pushed on it, but it barely moved. "What a struggle learning is, to get it not only into my head, but into my body and into my hands and actions… To feel it. Why can't I just download this into my brain?"

"If you could just download it, you would not have the satisfaction and enjoyment of learning and conquering, with the sheer bliss that comes from getting it. It's time to make a decision: Stay where you are, or take this new path and go over and around the obstacles, slashing down the thorns and debris that stand in your way. You can only grow with forward motion."

At that moment, I realized that Peacemaker had taken me past my expectations and my doubts. He was right. Learning is not always fun. But it is very necessary for my growth. That is good. And at the end of the day, it really is my decision.

I stood up straight and tall and I took one last look at the easy road, which seemed almost sepia in color. It did not grab or hold my attention any more. I looked again at the big gate that was filled with definition and color, daunting but alive, drawing me inexorably forward. "I do not know how. I am not even sure that I can. But remembering the look that Sharka gave me with his big eyes, it was as if he had told me, 'there is a way'. I know I have to try and find it."

The look Sharka gave me seemed to pierce my mind's eye. I closed my eyes and was instantly in a different place. I met myself face-to-face, part of me full of fear and doubt. I wanted to turn around and run away from the pressure of decision or having to push myself. The other part of me wanted to hold that gaze of Sharka's for longer, to connect to that feeling of living free and in the moment, of wanting to expand myself and transform into the thing that I wanted so badly to become, but was so afraid to try and grasp for, in case I failed miserably and had to live with myself being a failure.

Something within me stirred. It was as though my heart was warmed with assurance, certain that I would be okay, that I would be looked after, that my horse would be with me and show me the way, that it was okay to go forward with the fear. I nodded with agreement. With peace, I opened my eyes and said to Peacemaker, "Let's do it. Let's get through these gates. Somehow."

Peacemaker reared with delight and came close to me, rubbing his head up and down my side. "Thanks," I said, giggling as I was almost pushed off my feet. "Thanks for sharing this journey with me and helping me to discover so much. I... I really appreciate it," I said pressing my lips together and trying to hold back the tears.

Peacemaker held his head against my side for a few moments while I regained my composure.

"Now what? That is a gate that I do not know how to move."

Peacemaker looked at the gate with me. "There is a way. We just have to find it. Maybe it is like a voice sensor gate."

"Open sesame!" I yelled. Nothing happened. "Maybe there is a key somewhere."

We looked at the lock again, studying its strange shape. "This is big enough to fit my hand into," I said with curiosity. I began to connect the dots, putting my hand forward. I reached into the lock, but nothing happened. "Oh well, it was worth a try," I said, pulling my hand out.

"Hold on," Peacemaker said. "I have an idea. Try again, but when your hand is in the lock, turn it palm down and then lift it up."

"Palm down and lift it up?"

"Yes, like you are raising your hand and saying, 'Yes, I will take on the challenge'."

I placed my hand back in the lock, turning my palm down, then lifting up. I heard a big creaking and whirring sound, and a big click as the lock dropped open.

"That did it!" I said with hope and excitement. I pulled my hand out and placed the heavy lock on the ground. "Yahoo! Let's go!"

I took the massive chain off the gates and then pushed on one gate. But it didn't open easily, as I expected. I got in a better position and pushed harder, using everything that I had. Still nothing. "Huh," I sighed.

Gate of Decision

"Let me help," Peacemaker suggested as he pushed his shoulder to the gate.

Together, we counted, "One, two, three. PUSH!" and pushed hard on the cool metal frame. A big creak echoed as the gate slowly started to move forward. Keeping the momentum we had, we pushed again, just enough for both of us to squeeze through the opening.

"Whew, we made it! Thanks, Peacemaker," I said, with tears welling up in my eyes at the breakthrough I was able to just make. "It really is worth it to push through something. You do feel incredible after you have achieved each step. But even better, sometimes we need friends in our lives to help us to keep going, to give us encouragement."

"You are most welcome," he replied.

"We conquered the gate!" I yelled, elated, passionate, and full of energy.

"You made a decision to have a life that is more than just plain and easy."

"Yes, I did," I responded with pride. "I couldn't have done it without you."

Peacemaker winked and seemed to grin.

The glow of my necklace turned our attention to a new chapter of my life...

When the Student is Ready...

My friend was ready on the video camera, the battery fully charged and a new tape inserted. She shouted, "Okay, go!" as she pushed the record button. I was ready, pleased to be filmed so that I could submit a Level One tape, remembering with satisfaction the Level One that I thought would be impossible when I first looked at the brochure at the clinic.

My energy was really high. Being on camera always seemed to take me to another level of *I need to be perfect*, which added to my nervousness.

My friend juggled the roles of filming and of reading the sheet of the tasks we had to show. "Friendly game," she shouted. I started to flick the stick and string around Sharka. This game had improved greatly and Sharka now kept his feet still and tolerated the motion as I moved my feet all around his body and flicked the stick and string on the ground and over his back in a strong rhythm.

My necklace flashed us away from the scene back to the forest. As I stood by Peacemaker, I recounted the rest of the story to him.

"My friend called out each task for the Level One assessment and then I did my best attempt at showing each task. At the end we were both pleased with the filming and I was able to put the assessment tape together and send it off. It felt so good completing those Level One tasks that I had thought were initially impossible and unachievable when I had read about them at the clinic."

My necklace flashed and moved to a new scene.

"Hi! I am a Parelli instructor in New Zealand," the voice said from the other end of the phone line.

"Hi there," I replied as my energy lifted inside.

"I received your Level One tape and I wanted to talk to you about it. You did a great job," she encouraged in a warm, friendly tone.

"Thanks," I replied, feeling pleased and relieved.

"There are just a few things that need tweaking and explaining."

"What needs tweaking?" I asked.

Without directly answering the question, she replied, "I live in Nelson on the South Island, but I'm coming up to your area next month and I could give you a private lesson. We could run through a few things on your assessment, if you would like."

"Great! I would love that," I said excitedly. Having someone to actually help me and answer all my questions sounded like heaven. "When are you coming up?"

My necklace pulled us out of that scene and rapidly took us into a new one.

I saw myself at Pukekohe, New Zealand with my horse brushed and shining. My notes and questions sat in the corner of the barn on a chair. I peeked around the corner at the driveway for only the 15th time in the last 5

minutes in anticipation of meeting my instructor. My stomach started to get nervous as a car finally pulled up.

My necklace brought me back. "I remember that day so clearly."

"Fill me in on the rest of the story," Peacemaker encouraged.

"We had the lesson of a lifetime. Not only did I need a little tweaking, in some tasks I had no idea what I was doing. I felt a little stupid at times when she showed what they were really after, compared to what I was doing. They didn't have a lot of correlation. It's amazing how many people can read the same words on a piece of paper and take a different meaning from the same thing!

"My embarrassment of my misinterpretation of some of the tasks quickly turned to blame at the lack of clarity and information that the program had at the time. All this quickly dissipated as I was helped to clear up so many things. I was grateful to get the one-on-one help to set me up in the right direction. The results that came from it were amazing."

"What were the funny interpretations?" Peacemaker asked.

"One of the funniest things I remember from the filming and then the lesson were some obvious mistakes. Picture this... I have a task clear in my head; I know what I'm meant to do. My friend calls out the assignment. I walk a completely straight line, doing everything I am meant to with my hands, but the horse is not doing anything.

"She must have had a great laugh when she saw that, because at our lesson she pointed out that I had done the hand and rein positions very well. I just had one major thing missing. The horse was not yielding. I was extremely embarrassed when it was pointed out. But it is rather amusing now."

Peacemaker, goofing around, started prancing and then showing me his stuff. "Straight line, yielding, turning, etcetera. Is this what you were after?"

"You are such a show off."

"Takes one to know one."

My necklace flashed again.

It was a beautiful summer day, with only a few clouds in the sky. I was riding Sharka in another lesson with my instructor. The sand was flicking up, hitting the guardrail out of Sharka's hooves as we trotted around the arena.

"Rachel, I want you to hold a casual rein," she directed me.

I continued around the arena with my hands together, holding the reins in a fist with palms down, knuckles forward, and my reins still short. She asked, "Have I explained to you what a casual rein is?"

"No, not really," I replied, thinking it is what the picture looks like. *Maybe I needed to have a casual look on my face*, I thought to myself.

"It is where you hold the buckle of your reins and let them drape loosely with no contact on the bit."

I looked over with a *you have got to be joking* look on my face, and said politely with a knot forming in my stomach at the thought, "This horse does not go without holding the reins or he will really go and we will be miles away from here after he takes off."

"Your horse will learn to not take off, and will maintain his responsibility of not changing gait. Why don't we just try it and see how we go."

"Okay," I said, thinking that this will be interesting to show her how my horse goes without reins. Feeling uneasy and forgetting to breathe, I let the reins go, just a little bit. As I expected, Sharka helped me prove that he had no concept of going without contact on the reins. His speed picked up into a trot, then a canter in half the space of the arena, without me knowingly asking for it. I grabbed the reins back up short and tight and got him to stop. Then, with an uptight and *see it can't work* voice, I said, "See, this horse cannot do this."

Coming over to where we were standing, my instructor said calmly, "I believe that you can do this. We just need to start small until you both trust each other."

I started to breathe again. With a bit of disbelief, I listened. My fear and proving that it couldn't work seemed to fade when I realized that she genuinely just wanted to help me. She believed that we could do it. "I could start small," I said with a glimmer of hope forming.

"Great," she replied.

"So what do I do next?"

After hearing the explanation of the steps to achieving a casual rein and that a horse can maintain his responsibility, I felt assured that there was a way.

Peacemaker and I were once again back in the forest, the necklace fading back to silver.

"Thank goodness for people who have the dedication and ability to teach and help people to get on the right track," I said, and then smiled as I continued. "I admired her method of teaching and wanted to be an instructor just like her. She had a great style with horses and people. I was not an easy student, as I really did not understand some of the concepts or see how they were the building blocks in the foundation to be able to do anything that you want with a horse."

"What do you mean you were not an easy student?" Peacemaker asked.

I thought for a moment. "Well, I guess I was fearful."

"Fearful? What were you afraid of?"

"I was afraid of getting it wrong, of not moving forward. If I was really honest, I was afraid that it wouldn't work or I wouldn't be able to get it to work and that would shatter my dreams. That single thought seemed to lock me up and stop me from being open to new ideas.

"When I was given smaller steps to take to get there, I was able to trust her directives and move forward through the fear and make progress. And it wasn't just her excellent help. Sharka constantly helped me to not be overwhelmed and just concentrate on the one thing that we were playing with. He mirrored me a lot. He reacted to things just like I do. He was trying to show me a piece of who I was, not that I could clearly see that at the time. As I started to believe and open my heart to the possibilities, I made changes. Then he mirrored me and did the same."

"Did that help you to do anything that you wanted with Sharka?"

"I guess it did. Sharka and I achieved many dreams of mine together."

"Yes, you did."

I heard a whisper in my head as my necklace seemed to encourage me, drawing us a new picture.

A few white, fluffy clouds hovered in the warm summer sky. I was excited to try something new that day, something that I had never done before. Sharka was

saddled and warmed up, and I had set up two blue barrels five feet apart with a pole resting across the top of them. The ground was perfect, not too hard or too soft, with grass covering the area.

Anticipation built inside of me as I sat in a saddle atop Sharka. His bridle-less head faced the fence straight on about three strides away.

I took in a deep, soft breath and reveled in the realization that our trust and partnership had grown more than I had imagined. I had dreamed of doing what I was about to do with Sharka since the first time I watched the video of Pat riding around and jumping with nothing on his horse's head.

Having never done this, I felt apprehensive. I lifted my energy and asked Sharka for a canter. He responded quickly and sprang forward. One, two, three strides and we lifted up and sailed over the fence effortlessly, seeming to hang in the air for a very long time. One, two more strides and we slowed down, and at three strides we stopped. I asked him to turn an indirect rein (turn on the forehand), which he did softly to face the way we had just come from. He relaxed, while my energy bubbled with excitement.

Delighted, a big smile spread across my face. But we were not finished yet. With even more confidence, I raised my energy again and focused past the fence. I asked again for the canter, and Sharka sprang forward from a halt. One, two, three, jump. The jump was big enough that I had to lean quite far forward to stay balanced as Sharka sat back then sprang up as we glided through the air. I moved my weight back as we landed.

Sharka's athleticism and style over the fence made it a smooth transition. We took our three strides after the fence, then stopped and turned to face the other direction, resting and relaxing.

"Yes!" I said as I threw my arms up into the air. Tears of joy were streaming down my face. It was a moment I would never forget. I might as well have won the Olympics.

"We did it!" Elated, I threw my hands up in the air again. "Yahoo!" Then I gave Sharka a great big hug, reveling in the moment, a euphoric feeling buzzing through my veins. We had achieved something together that I had only dared to hope and dream for.

Then my mind ran through Sharka's history. An ex-racehorse turned jumper, he had been fearful, frightened, and panicked. When he was given to me, I had no idea how to mold this horse to become a partner and teammate.

I shook my head with astonishment, remembering my first ride and all the frustrations that we had been through. We were reaping the rewards of moving forward and sticking with the program, learning new things and going to places I had never been before. I was aglow, the memory etched into my mind forever.

I looked around to double check. There was no one to witness this grand occasion.

"Yahoo! The horse that I could hardly stop with two reins, that scared me with his power, turned around!" I was back in the forest with Peacemaker, still cheering the scene of my memory. "That was so incredibly cool. I am having trouble even expressing what that meant. I wish I had that on film, or a picture, or anything."

"Maybe it just makes it all the more special that there was no one around and there is no record," Peacemaker suggested.

"I guess," I replied wistfully. "This momentous event helped me to come to a big decision. I was not satisfied with my 40-hour a week office job. Instead, I was inspired by what Natural Horsemanship was helping me achieve. I wanted to know more, and to teach others. Teaching what I had just done was a dream job to me. Helping others to find out how cool this program is and what you learn about yourself from it, and what inspiring things you can do with a horse, is something I wanted to learn more about.

"I was forever changed. A piece of me dared to dream. I wanted to quit my job, turn to something new. I had enough hope to try. The changes were not just with my horsemanship. It was a heart change. I opened up and let myself be vulnerable. Instead of shattering if I didn't get it right, I felt a restoration as I learned to be in the moment, to be alive and experience the ups and downs of learning and still move forward.

"Sometimes it pushed me to the edge of what I thought I could cope with. I wanted to really help other people heal their hearts, with the horse as a guide and a facilitator.

"I had not really thought about it like that before. I guess deep down I just really wanted to help people."

Can I Jump?

Peacemaker nodded in agreement. "Yes, that is what you wanted to do, and you wanted more healing for yourself as well. So, what did you do to follow your dream?"

"At that time, I never really wanted to travel or explore the world. I loved it right where I was."

"Then you suddenly had a great reason?"

"Yes. The successes I was having gave me hope of increasing my horsemanship skills, of changing my job to something I loved. I had to have more.

"I got really brave and applied to travel to the U.S. and become a working student, which was completely out of character for me. There is always a way. I couldn't afford to pay for a class over there, but if I was a working student, I could learn and pay my way.

"I sent in the application and waited, not actually having to make any huge decisions or do anything out of the ordinary – unless I got accepted."

"You were waiting for an answer before you had to actually do anything about it?"

"Yep."

As we had continued to walk, I had been so engrossed in our conversation that I hadn't noticed the landscape having dramatically changed. I realized that we had been walking upward for some time.The majesty of the canyon that suddenly spread before us seemingly out of nowhere was awe-inspiring. The depth and size was magnificent. When you see those things in the movies or in pictures, they are amazing. But somehow actually being near what you've only seen from a distance brings it to life, and it moves your spirit.

I looked around, ensuring that I didn't get too close to the edge. Soaking up the beauty of this picturesque view, I observed the massive rocks, their sheer size making me feel small, appreciative of nature and its strength and power.

Looking down into the canyon, everything looked so small. The energy that nature feeds you is amazing. Smelling the fresh air, I let out a breath, feeling satisfied and content in the surroundings.

Peacemaker, standing beside me, asked, "Are you ready to take the next challenge in your quest?" My entire body froze with the realization that there was another challenge.

"My next mission? What do you mean? I tackled a waterfall on my last mission, and then there were the gates. That was big. I'm not sure I'm up for another mission," I blurted out, my brain spinning with the new information.

Peacemaker calmly responded, "To live where nothing holds you back is going to require you to face your fears, and do things you have never done before."

I really didn't like the sound of this 'face your fears' talk. "Maybe it is much better to just let your fears be, and enjoy life a little." Then I remembered the gate of change. "Face your fears," I whispered to myself.

Peacemaker's silence was driving me wild, and my curiosity got the better of me. "Well, okay. What do you mean? What is this next challenge?"

"Your next challenge is about trusting while facing a fear. I am going to ask you to do something that you think is impossible. But I know that you can do it."

The words, "I know you can do it" gave me a huge sense of relief, enabling me to stay open as I listened intently.

"All you need to do is trust that you will be looked after." Then after a few moments, he revealed the challenge. "Jump off this ledge," Peacemaker said calmly.

I forced out a laugh, as I waited for Peacemaker to relent. He just held my gaze. Then I realized he was serious.

"Yeah, right," I replied with disbelief. Peacemaker continued to hold a steady gaze, staying silent as he waited for me to grasp that this challenge was real.

"I am serious," Peacemaker insisted, angling his nose back so his face was looking down at me, with 'I mean it' written all over it. I recognized the serious look.

I felt like a big heavy fishing net had just fallen on me, holding me down, while a voice inside me said, *You have to do this*. My feet felt stuck to the ground. "I don't want to drop off that edge," I started to say. "I don't even want to get close to it, for that matter. Why would I?"

"Because you want to live where nothing holds you back."

Remembering the quest and the reason for being here, I sighed. "Okay, you have got my attention." My feet might be ready to move, but I still felt like a net was

over me all the same. "There must be some other thing I can do. I am not going to be an idiot and just jump off a ledge because you say it will help me."

"This is life-changing time. This is the time to meet your fears face-to-face and conquer them once and for all."

"Help me understand how jumping off this edge blindly and hoping that I live after I have faced my fears helps me? I guess I would be cured of fear, but dead. What good does that do?"

"If you jump off that edge, I can promise you great change and wonder, new levels of trust, and starting to live your life with nothing holding you back. If you stay here, you will *not* live where nothing holds you back, and you will *not* complete your destiny."

Hearing the stakes and the two loud "nots" that Peacemaker had emphasized, and what was on the line, I replied, "Well that makes me want to do it, but look Peacemaker, unlike a lot of people, I am not interested in Bungee jumping or jumping out of an airplane with a parachute, or anything crazy and wild like that. So you are talking to the wrong person with this challenge."

Peacemaker ignored my backchat and replied, "What if I told you that your life will never be the same if you are willing to take this leap? That it will open up a whole new world of possibilities?"

"I love the idea, but I'm afraid to do it."

Peacemaker softened, knowing that he was getting to my core fears. He asked, "What are you afraid of?"

"Falling, dying... getting it wrong, not being perfect, not having the things I have dreamed and wished for."

Peacemaker rested his nose on my shoulder and I could feel his warm breath intermittently on my neck.

Can I Jump?

"What if I said you can have it all if you will only believe and trust that all things are possible. What do you have to lose?"

"You are right. I have nothing to lose," I replied, at the same time doubting the words that came out of my mouth.

"Do you trust me?" Peacemaker asked.

"I do trust you."

"Do you believe that I would give you a task if I thought that you could not do it?"

"No, I don't think that you would ask me to do anything that was not possible. But I really do not see how this is possible," I replied with emotion and emphasis.

"Now we are getting to the core issues. What if I told you, you are not alone? What if I went with you? Will you go with me? Can you see that it is possible if you have someone to go with?"

I felt a surge of hope that it would be okay if Peacemaker were to go with me. *He won't kill himself*, I said to myself. "Yes, I do," I responded to his last query.

I turned for a moment, walking to the edge of the ledge and looking down at the sheer drop. I thought, *This is crazy. But what if I could do it?* My brain buzzed with conflicting thoughts, my emotions in a twirl as they switched from dread to trust to confidence to trepidation. How would I feel if I walked away from this opportunity? Would I always wish I had given it a try? I would never know if I didn't try. I would always wonder, *What if?* I can imagine lying on my deathbed, looking back over my life and regretting not having taken a challenge that would take me to the next level. I didn't want regrets. I wanted to conquer my fears. I

wanted to know that it is worth pushing to the next level. I decided I had no choice but to do it.

I turned back to Peacemaker, who was waiting patiently, and said, "Okay, I will do it with you."

"Great," he replied as he bowed down for me to climb on his back.

I yelled, "I believe!" As he stood up, I realized that I was shaking with fear. I yelled again, "I believe!" with Peacemaker joining me.

We took off in a gallop toward the edge. My fear flashed right in front of me. I gripped tightly to Peacemaker's sides, wondering if I should bail? Was I crazy? Then I remembered that I trusted and I believed, and I was going to face my fear, believing everything is possible.

I looked out toward the horizon and held on tight. Peacemaker reached the edge and jumped. I felt his body lift and I leaned forward, closing my eyes for a moment as if that would help me not have to face what might happen next. I hoped that there was a magical bridge that couldn't be seen, or a ledge that we would stop on. But I could feel a breeze on my face and ears, the moments seeming to go by too long for a gravitational drop. I opened my eyes and, to my surprise, we were not on a ledge or a bridge, or falling down. We were still moving forward, straight ahead.

I heard a soft whooshing sound and felt air behind me. I looked down and saw two great big white wings. We were flying! Peacemaker had wings!

"Wow, you didn't tell me about your wings!" I exclaimed, my emotions whirling with absolute delight and enchantment. "How amazing!"

Can I Jump?

Peacemaker laughed, "I did leave that part out, didn't I? But, you would not have pushed through your fears. Knowing that it was going to be okay, there would be no fear. Well, maybe a little. But sometimes you have to do things with the fear of not knowing if it is going to work or not."

Still high from my adrenaline buzz, I could see Peacemaker's point. I had this incredible feeling that I was unstoppable. "Yahoo, I believe!" I shouted as we glided through the sky, breathing in the fresh, clean smell of outdoors as we flew through the air.

I felt a sense of real accomplishment that I had done it. I pushed through my fears and I felt stronger and more confident for doing it.

We soared for a while checking out the landscape. I could see a river moving along its chiseled path, the tops of trees following the river's edge. Meadows and clearings sprang up full of lush spring grass. The sides of the canyon were chiseled with colorful shades of rock.

"Okay, that's where we are going to land," Peacemaker said as he headed toward a small open clearing near the river. He gently touched the ground.

Our delight was doubled by the sound of water. I hopped off Peacemaker and we both ran to the edge for a drink. Cupping my hand and filling it with cool, clear water, I lifted it to my mouth. The fresh liquid was tonic to my soul. I reached down again and even the second handful hardly touched the sides as it flew down my throat. "Oh, I needed that."

"Me too," Peacemaker agreed between drinks as he licked his lips.

"That was a pretty extreme way of helping me face my fears. But what a huge shift I feel in my spirit!"

"Like you can really believe that all things are possible now?"

"Yes, I can trust that I can put it all on the line and be okay."

"Tell me more," Peacemaker encouraged.

"Well, that really pushed my fear of faith, belief, and hope. That I could go beyond my seen and understood capabilities. I feel reassured that I am looked after, and I can go forward."

"Speaking of going forward, you were accepted into the working student program weren't you?"

"Yes. It was pretty scary and exciting all at the same time," I added, remembering that feeling buzzing inside me, and the thoughts running through my mind, like, *What in the heck are you doing? Are you crazy?*

"The other side of the world," Peacemaker interrupted my thoughts. "That was a pretty big risk, leaving your full time, secure office job and going to the U.S."

I thought a moment. "I guess that was pretty huge. In fact, bigger than I even thought. I would not have called myself a risk-taker, but that was certainly a big one, leaving my job and income. The decision was not an easy one to make. The scarcity and fear inside me certainly gave me some pushback, and made me not want to take the plunge. I struggled with that decision for awhile."

"So wanting to help others and your heart change, did that help you take the leap?"

"Yes, I guess subconsciously, but no, I didn't really get that at the time. I just thought it was for progress, more change. The Parelli progam had already assisted me to make massive changes with my horse. I was almost Level Three in their system, and I wanted more. I wanted to be the best I could be. At that time, I mainly thought I just wanted to be good with horses, and if going overseas was the way, then I would do it. The 'I have to change my life and grow' in me won the battle, just like the jump we just took. Now that I had a good taste of this, I couldn't keep living how I was. I knew that there was more out there to learn, and I wanted more. I wanted it in a big dose and the sooner the better. I wanted change. I had to take the leap. I had learned so much, but I wanted immersion."

Peacemaker interrupted, jokingly saying, "There glows your necklace."

The hustle and bustle of Auckland Airport in New Zealand was in full swing with many people milling around, the loud speakers overhead reminding me that I was in a public place, and no help in feeling relaxed or at ease.

We went upstairs to the area where passengers only pass through the gate with a boarding pass. My family and friends had come to wish me off. Part of me didn't want to leave them. Another part of me was excited. I was buzzing and scared about this new adventure, and my stomach churned with nervousness. A thought buzzed through my head: *What am I doing?*

Luckily, my heart affirmed: *The right thing.*

The turmoil made me feel deeply vulnerable and I couldn't hold back the tears as I kissed and hugged everyone, then waved goodbye. My feet were sticky and slow, not knowing what the future was to hold, and missing everyone already.

I walked through the final gates, still wondering what on earth I was doing. But I was doing it all the same. One last big wave at my family and friends, then I was out of

sight. With a big sigh, I said in my head, *Here I go.* I walked forward and headed to the security line.

"I can still feel the apprehension and excitement and whirling emotions right now. That was a big day."

My necklace glowed again.

Plane ride number one was done. I had made it across the ocean and entered the United States of America, incredibly excited to be there and a little offended at being called an "alien" when we passed through immigration.

I walked through the terminal to find my next gate. I found the voices of all the people around me talking exceptionally loud. The American accent stood out in my groggy head, still fuzzy from the 12-hour night flight from New Zealand. All the same, it tickled me. I giggled to myself, with a big smile on my face. *They talk so funny over here,* I thought to myself.

A guy in a cowboy hat walking through the airport caught my attention. *Wow, people actually wear those in public here!* I had never seen it before. I thought they were just for the movies and shows, or maybe just for cowboys with horses. I smiled and laughed inwardly as I saw another great big hat. What a funny thing. They looked so out of place from what I was used to. They weren't on horseback or on a farm. This was really quite different.

"Cowboy hats are such a funny thing. I have tried over the years to wear one, but they just do not work for me at all. I sort of have this mental block with them."

"What about me?" Peacemaker asked as he stood under some leaves that looked a lot like a hat.

Laughing, I replied, "I think it works really well on you."

"Go on. You are just saying that," Peacemaker joked.

Can I Jump?

"You are right, I was. I like you just the way you are."

"There goes that necklace again."

Feeling like a small child in a new adventure in wonderland, we made the drive to the Parelli International Study Centre in Pagosa Springs, Colorado. On the way, the taxi driver pointed out a real live bear out in a field on the side of the road. This big brown bear was just wandering around near the trees in full sight. The wilds of America! I didn't realize that bears would be just wandering around out there.

Gulping in my surroundings, I couldn't believe how dry the landscape was compared to New Zealand's green. There was grass, but not covering every inch of the dry red soil. Some of the buildings were made out of logs stacked on top of each other. What a different style.

I was filled with excitement as we made our way up the drive to the Centre. Looking around, my gaze stopped at the big snowcapped Rocky Mountains. They were breathtaking to look at. I was amazed how much the altitude at 7500 feet affected me as I walked up a small hill to take a better look at where we were. I was quickly out of breath.

There was an adjoining forest behind the Centre, but unlike New Zealand, you could see through the trees, and the brush was not thick and rainforest-like. I was looking forward to exploring more, but night came far too quickly, and I was tired enough from the trip that even with all of the excitement and the newness of this place, I went to sleep very quickly.

My necklace flashed us to a new scene.

That summer came and went much more quickly than I realized. I was mixed about wanting it to end and not wanting it to end. Another student from New

Zealand had left a few days earlier and had gotten her Level Three. So I was hopeful and expecting that I would get mine, too.

The end of summer get-together was in full swing, and the awards portion was under way. We all cheered and clapped as each student went up and received the awarded level they had achieved. I was expectant and waiting for my turn.

The awards section finished, and I was not even mentioned. I felt like someone had punched me in the stomach, my head had a buzz in it, and my breathing quickened. I almost felt sick. My disappointment grew as they wrapped up the awards and I did not get anything.

I wasn't quite sure what to do with myself. Should I run away and find a place to hide? It must have been obvious. I was incredibly disillusioned and unsure why this had happened.

After I got over the initial shock and pulled myself together, I went to find one of the Protégés who had been instructing us.

"I was wondering why I didn't get my Level Three? What do you need to see? What can I show you?" I asked.

"There is nothing I need to see. You need to ask Pat."

Not wanting to ask Pat, I found another Protégé. "What do you need to see?" I asked.

"Don't ask me. I think you are Level Three. Ask Pat."

I guess there was nothing left to do but to ask Pat. So I took in a deep breath and walked up to the table where he was sitting, and waited my turn to talk with him. I sat down and asked, "Pat, I was wondering what you needed to see from me to pass my Level Three?"

Can I Jump?

Pat did not directly answer the question. Instead, he asked me, "Who was your instructor?"

"There are no instructors in New Zealand who assess Level Three. I have had lots of lessons and clinics with two of your top Australian instructors, one of whom has also been assessing my Level Three."

"Okay, I will chat with them when I am down there in a few months about a few things," he answered.

"Okay," I replied. "Thanks," I added, still confused and unsure of what I could do, as I got up and left the table. I guess that was all I was going to find out. I was incredibly disappointed, and did not see any way I could do anything to pass this level of certification.

I was upset. *Five months, and I didn't get what I came for*, buzzed through my head as my frustration rose, with no clear ability to change the circumstances. I had set my hopes on this and now the time was over and I felt a huge nothing, a void as my emotions swirled back and forth. I was unable to do anything about the situation and unclear of what to do and where to go next.

"Had your back against the wall there, huh?"

I jumped as Peacemaker's voice jolted me back to reality. "You bet. I was blessed when I got some peace from some words of wisdom from a visiting instructor from Australia. He gave me some hope to hold onto."

"Do tell."

"He told me that I should not worry. That I was Level Three, and that Pat was just checking out my emotional fitness. I hoped this was true and held onto those words. At the same time, my emotional fitness was not feeling that good at all." I paused. "Peacemaker, to be honest, I felt like a failure spending a whole summer in the States at the source, and not achieving one of my main goals. It

was embarrassing to go home and say, 'Well, my friend got her Level Three, and I didn't'," I said, dejectedly.

"I bet," Peacemaker agreed.

"You know, I had such high hopes. I put it all on the line, sold everything I had of value, left my job. I wanted something so much more than ordinary. I wanted something amazing, different, new. The first month did not turn out at all as I had expected. We did nothing but work, clean up rubbish, fix fences, feed horses, clean cabins, dig ditches, and more, preparing for the summer and the paying students' arrival. The team of us working on these projects had fun together and relationships grew quickly. But there was no horsemanship at all, no learning, no nothing. It was a little frustrating, to say the least."

The scene captured our attention again.

"Why can't we play with a horse?" I asked the ranch manager.

"Because the ground is so wet we don't want to ruin the arena surfaces. And we want to wait for Pat to arrive."

"Oh great," I replied with chagrin. *Pat is not expected for another week*, I said to myself with disappointment.

I turned my attention back to Peacemaker and continued our conversation. "Those four weeks without horses to play with put quite a damper on the entire experience. I picked up a lot of angst. My feet started to drag, questions popped up in my mind. *'What am I doing here? I could be playing with my horse at home. I could be…'*

"I could be anywhere but there. I was pretty upset and had my expectations dashed. But, things are not always as they seem. I thought that I had been cheated out of something somehow at the time. But in hindsight it was just the way it was meant to be. I mean, they could have explained what was going to happen right away. Then you are prepared for it. But it wasn't so bad. It is always interesting when you look back on your life or a situation, how it can appear so different than what it felt like in the moment."

"It all depends on which glasses you were wearing," Peacemaker replied.

Startled by his out of the ordinary reply, I asked, "What glasses I was wearing?"

Enchanted Glasses

"Step this way." Peacemaker urged me to where he was standing. On the other side of the tree, sitting magically in rows were glasses of every shape and size and color, neatly resting on racks. I counted five pair across and eight pair down.

Enamored, I scanned the different glasses. Peacemaker casually said, "Try the black pair on in row three, two in from the left."

I reached forward and picked up a large square pair of glasses with thick frames, not liking the look or the way they felt as I turned them around and placed them on my head.

"Oh my gosh, the picture is dim." I looked around and as I spun my head I was amazed at what I could see that I had not even noticed before. "The mold on that tree is really gross. Now I can even smell it. There are lots of shadows in here around the trees. Was that a black horse?" My eyes followed a dark shadow that looked like a horse, but it seemed to vanish as quickly as it appeared, and there wasn't anything there.

I felt the hair stand up on the back of my neck, the glasses pressing into the side of my head. I jumped to avoid the huge spider I saw out of the corner of my eye. I ripped the glasses from my face and winced.

"These glasses are not very good at all, Peacemaker," I said as I threw them to the ground.

"They are exactly what they are meant to be. Read the label inside the frame," he suggested.

I tentatively picked them up, holding them away from me as if I might catch something. I turned them and read the label out loud. "'The dark, shady world around.' That makes more sense. They definitely show you all the dark, scary things."

"Try the glasses two rows down and four across."

I counted 1, 2 and 1, 2, 3, 4. They had food around the rims that actually looked good enough to eat. Not about to jump straight in this time, I read the label first: 'Everything is edible.'

"Okay," I said, intrigued, tilting my head to the side. As I positioned them over my ears, the whole world looked different, particularly appetizing. "Oh my gosh, that tree looks delicious. Maybe I should try some. Oh, look at that grass!" Everything had taken on a 3-D appearance, with light and color. I felt like I had just walked into a fairytale where everything was made of food.

I raced forward to grab something to eat, not sure where to start. Peacemaker, seeing that I had gotten completely carried away, picked his front leg up, extending it in front of me to stop me. I tripped, and as I fell forward my arms cushioned the fall. The glasses fell off my head and tumbled to the ground.

"Ow!" I said and I realized that we were still in the woods. Coming to my senses, I turned to Peacemaker.

"Thanks. I guess I needed that." I stood and brushed myself off. "I will just return these to their home."

As I put the food glasses back, Peacemaker suggested, "Try the bright pink glasses on the bottom, far right."

"Okay. Oh wow, these give out a different tint," I said while placing them on my head and looking around. "These glasses are amazing. I see my life and what I have done and achieved. It is incredible! I am so blessed and lucky to be alive."

"Look at the label on the glasses you are wearing."

I pulled them off and read the label: 'Thankfulness.'

"Wow, these glasses all really do work. They help you to focus on different things, and there are all sorts here," I said, letting my fingers run down the rows.

"Remember which ones you are still wearing. These are all yours, but you often choose which ones you wear without even realizing it consciously. Some of them are not easy to take off," Peacemaker explained.

"You are right," I said, realizing what Peacemaker had just said. "These are my glasses and I choose which ones I am going to wear, what I am going to focus on."

"Try these," Peacemaker said, encouraging me to explore the uniqueness of each of the glasses, picking up a cute iridescent blue pair with his teeth. The glasses seemed to just glide onto my face.

"Wow, the colors look more alive. These are awesome. I love these. You look amazing, Peacemaker!" I exclaimed.

"That's exactly why I gave you those. It is amazing how good I look when you have those on," Peacemaker teased, winking as he turned so I could get a peek at his better side.

Enchanted Glasses

I laughed at his joke, then pausing, asked, "So, am I in control of which glasses I pick up?"

"Yes, you are. It is amazing how much control you have over what you focus on and see, without even realizing it."

Distracted, I placed the blue pair back and reached for another distinctly small pair of green glasses. "Wow, these are cool. Everything is sooooo tall, and I am a midget," I said as I placed them back and grabbed a large yellow pair next to the green pair. "Now these I like. I am huge and everything else is really small. I could just push this tree over I am so big and strong."

I reached over to the tree. Peacemaker interrupted me, "Come on you. Over here."

I pulled the glasses off and returned to my usual size.

"These are the glasses we need now." Peacemaker put his nose on a pair.

I picked them up and the label read: 'See the positive.' I paused. "Sounds good to me." I put the glasses on.

"Now tell me about your experience at Parelli Centre. You were like a cat out of water," Peacemaker jibed.

"I was certainly surprised by how different things were. Quite a shock to the system, for sure. I met lots of really nice people and had quite a few adventures. I rode lots of horses and watched some excellent demonstrations from Pat and Linda. I watched students doing courses, too. But looking back, the real growth came from washing dishes, cleaning toilets, feeding horses, cleaning cabins, and trying to keep a good attitude with that."

"So, how did that go for you?" Peacemaker asked.

"Not so well. In fact, my attitude was horrible. I have to say I was a little bitter about a few things that happened. Looking back with the new perspective these glasses give me, I can see that it was actually really good for me. I can clearly remember one day when Pat walked through the lodge and asked me what I was doing. I replied, 'Cleaning up after you lot.' He calmly replied, 'I resemble that remark.'

"I kept on walking as he moved off, but that comment really caught me off guard, and he hadn't taken my hostility or upset. I thought that was great. I have thought about that often."

"Life is often like that. Things can be much better in hindsight," Peacemaker affirmed.

"Oh yeah," I agreed with long emphasis on those two words. "But there was also a lot of fun stuff. Getting to know people from all over the world, hearing all the different dialects. We had some really great times trying to imitate them, as they did me.

"Riding in golf carts, going on fun trail rides in and out of the oak brush. Oh yeah, being taken down a steep sand slide on the side of a mountain on horseback. Now that was an adrenaline rush, as the horse is going straight down and your legs are nearly up by their ears while you try to stay in the saddle, and the ground is moving beneath the both of you. Whew, that was an emotional pusher. There was a lot of yahooing after that experience.

"Going to and soaking in the thermal pools in town. Great lessons from Pat's Protégés. Performing in the open house. Seeing bears in the garbage and in the horses' feed. The cutest chipmunks loving the horse grain. Oh yeah, and four girls sleeping in a cabin together with no electricity, just a propane heater. We all got to shower and eat down at the lodge. Playing pranks on some of the other working students. I won't go into that. It was really fun and a growth experience at what a group of us affectionately nicknamed Parelli camp.

"It looks a little different now, doesn't it?" Peacemaker asked.

"Wow. It really does. That was a fun adventure. Regardless of whether I received my Level Three or not."

"There is learning in everything. So what did you do next?"

"I returned home and shifted my focus to preparation for the upcoming tour stop in New Zealand in just two months. Sharka was amazing. After five months off, he didn't miss a beat. His fitness was low, but he was ready to play with me all the same. My savvy had increased much more than I realized. It was as if the things I had seen and experienced at the Centre started to become a part of me, like osmosis. I started to play with him and recognized that I had way more to offer him than I had before. He had a few lameness issues that held us back, but we were quickly on our way again in no time."

"Alright, I bet that was fun getting home and playing with everything that you had discovered."

"Yes, it was. I had new things to try, so my excitement for my horse grew.

"Speaking of focus, my necklace is gleaming. Must be a new piece of reality for us to see."

The Ti Papa Equestrian Centre in Auckland was abuzz with horse lovers. The crowd was excited to see more displays from Pat Parelli and the Savvy Team on Sunday, after having already been wowed the day before. Sharka was brushed up and shining, ready to go.

I love performing in front of people, even when I have butterflies and my energy is high.

The big indoor arena had seating set up all the way around a taped-off area. People were in plastic chairs and on hay bales or whatever they had brought to sit on. The music was playing popular and upbeat songs that really got me moving to the beat, helping me to concentrate on playing with my horse.

Sharka did so well in front of the crowd, sticking with me as we ran and stopped and played around. Intermittently, the crowd would clap when a combination in the Savvy Team did something cool with their horse. Sharka was excellent with the clapping, but being in front of the crowd was intense for him, and he stayed close by me. After we loosened up, we began to enjoy ourselves.

The music stopped and Pat came out into the arena and called the entire Savvy Team over, then asked Linda to come out.

"Linda has something to present," Pat explained. Linda walked up to me and presented me with my green 9' Savvy String, which reflected my passing my Level Three.

I whooped in a big breath of air and smiled, a little in shock, but absolutely delighted. "Thank you," I replied, a little bit stunned.

Pat said loudly, "Let's give our newest Level Three Graduate a hand!"

Everyone in the crowd gave me a big applause. With tears in my eyes and a feeling of overwhelm, I managed another "Thank you" to Linda, who held my hand as we shared a special moment in front of everyone. Pat excused us and we all left the arena, the tears still moist in my eyes while my beaming smile shined through.

I was thrilled. Achieving Level Three was a huge accomplishment, made all the better by being awarded in front of a home crowd, and from Pat and Linda personally presenting it to me.

"Alright, that is more like it," Peacemaker encouraged.

"Thanks. I needed that acknowledgment," I admitted.

"You didn't realize how cool that was, did you?" Peacemaker observed, seeing the tears in my eyes and the emotions that this new perspective gave me.

"No, I have to admit I was a bit bitter about feeling like a failure leaving the Centre in Colorado when I hadn't received my Level Three. I bet Pat and Linda really wanted to honor me for my dedication, and giving me my Level Three in front of a home crowd was a much higher honor than I would have felt receiving it earlier." I paused, and then was struck by a realization.

"I really didn't understand the high opinion that Pat and Linda had for me," I said in wonder. "I'm seeing now what a wonderful gift it was," I acknowledged, pulling off the glasses that Peacemaker had given me. "A change in perspective goes a long way. I'm learning to receive more in my life. The funny thing is that sometimes the things are already in your life, or the timing isn't what you expect. But they are there all the same. It is just learning to receive them that is the tricky part," I concluded.

"That is a great realization. I think your necklace has more to show you than just scenes," Peacemaker said knowingly.

"You are right," I agreed.

As we walked along, Peacemaker continued. "So tell me more about what happened?"

"After the tour stop, I was fired up, having received my Level Three. I applied to become a Parelli instructor, and was thrilled when I was accepted. Whizzing forward on that emotional high rollercoaster, I put it all on the line and packed my bags and went back to the Parelli University committed to study and learn more."

"What did it take to enable you to do that?" he inquired.

"The commitment was massive. I knew where I was going and what I would have to do to go to the next level. The financial cost was huge for me, but I was willing to risk it all. I had to leave my job again and sell my horse truck and pull everything I could together. Especially as the New Zealand dollar at that time was only 42 cents on the U.S. dollar. I used every last cent to make the next part of my dream come true."

"It wasn't about the money though, was it?"

"No, it was about stepping out to follow my dream."

"You had to take this step or fear staying in the same place or slipping back into the groove again."

"That's right," I said, realizing the truth in the wise words Peacemaker had given me. "In fact, I was surprised how supportive the people at my job were. I guess not too many people just leave everything to follow their dream."

"It is amazing what you can do when you want something. There is always a way, and you found it," he confirmed.

Peacemaker and I walked into a beautiful meadow. The grass smelled fresh, and I sat down to enjoy the sun and take a rest.

Enchanted Glasses

"So, tell me about your experience back at the university," Peacemaker encouraged as he bent his head to eat while he listened. I lay back in the grass and recounted my experience.

"What memories. It felt great to be back in Pagosa Springs, remembering the smells, seeing the diverse terrain, the beautiful snow-capped mountains. Oh, I had grown to really love that place, and enjoyed seeing my friends again. What an exciting summer, being a full-time student.

"The university brought a few new exciting challenges and pushed some of my limits. The announcement of a colt start the following week was a highlight. I had never started a horse before, and I was very nervous at the thought of learning this new skill. We learned all the things that the horses needed to know to give them a well-rounded education, and a good start. I really had to push past some of my own thresholds when getting on their back for the first time.

"I vividly remember one of the first rides we put on the colts. The whole class was freshly mounted in the coverall, a fairly small space for about 15 horses and people. Then one of the Protégés on the ground announced that he was going to move us all around as a herd, with a carrot stick and plastic bag, and we had to hope that our young colt would hold it together and not throw us away in the excitement.

"My shock at the whole idea was strong, but I had to hold it together and help my horse, even with the uneasiness and apprehension. The Protégé lifted the bag, which fluttered with a life of its own on the end of the straight fiberglass stick. The horses moved quickly away from the pressure, almost unaware of their humans on

top… or, incredibly aware of their humans on top, with the extra pressure an easy thing to flee from.

"The herd moved together and changed directions smoothly, much to my amazement and relief. I quickly started to enjoy the process and the way my colt handled the entire movement. There was only one horse that had trouble and he was with a very experienced rider who helped him through it.

"I moved to another level of confidence and understanding with horses as we learned some incredible skills. I had never thought that I would ever start a horse. I had always liked riding them when others were finished with them. But this experience changed my mind and gave me some new skills that set me up for life with horses."

"Sounds like you had an amazing time."

"Oh yes, I did."

"What happened next?"

"During the rest of the university, I rode six to eight horses a day and had lessons with Protégés and Pat and Linda. The university seemed to fly by all too quickly. I really didn't want to leave."

"You didn't leave, did you?"

"No. I talked with the management, and was thrilled when they offered me a position to stay on with them for another ten weeks. I was hooked. That time seemed to fly by all too quickly. And then I had to leave the country and get a new visa."

"So what happened to Sharka back in New Zealand?"

"Sharka. The name still brings a smile to my face." I paused for a moment, then a feeling of elation and joy wrapped around me. "You know, Peacemaker. We did it! Sharka and I really did it. We achieved what I had hoped and dreamed of, and in some ways, more than I expected. It all came together!" I exclaimed after a lightning bolt of realization struck me. I sat up, then stood up, holding my hands up while looking down with a stunned sensation, as if the world was spinning around me. "Wow, how did I not see it clearly until now?"

"There is a time and a place for everything. Playing with new glasses really helps you out, too," he teased. "Tell me more about it coming together with Sharka."

"Well... Sharka and I gave a free demo..." I started to say as my necklace zipped us away to the scene.

Sharka and I were both fit and ready for anything. His coat was shining in the beautiful summer day at the Waiuku Sunflower Festival in New Zealand. We were being introduced over the loud speaker,

My butterflies were in full force. I managed to get half of them traveling together, then the music came on and I was able to get the rest to fly in formation just as we ran out into the middle of the arena together. I could feel our bond and connection, sharing our energy and emulating each other.

Sharka and I had played those games and moves many times, but there was something special about showing others the beauty of them. It helped us shine and move in a new dimension of unison. Keeping Sharka's connection and presence seemed effortless, and surprising, with the many distractions that the fair had, with people, the next presentation of dogs, and the amusement park rides. Even with all of those things going on, we stayed focused and present in the moment. Blocking out the rest of the world and concentrating on our bond and what we were doing together came easily. We were in the moment, and when we were in that place

together, it was beautiful. It wasn't about what we could do or how we did it. It was about our connection, like being in an invisible bubble together. It felt amazing to be linked with him and to move and play together.

For a brief moment, I started to think about the crowd watching. They might see a few circles and sideways, going fast, then backing up. But they couldn't feel our bubble and the amazing and incredible feeling we were experiencing.

Sharka felt my change in energy and focus, and I sensed his energy and presence move away, too. He disconnected and ran toward the far fence. For a brief moment, I felt alone. Then with confidence, I followed him with high intensity and focused my energy on him. He felt me coming and gave me half an eye. I backed off a little, and he decided to reconnect. Taking all my focused energy off of him as he accepted my invitation, he ran back to me, the connection re-established. The feeling was great.

It was always amazing how he was so perceptive to my energy, movements, and connection. He knew me so well. He stopped when I stopped. He went when I went. It was just like a dance, an indescribable feeling of affinity.

As Peacemaker and I continued to watch, I asked Sharka to run up into the horse trailer at liberty. He knew this game well and ran up the ramp with enthusiasm. He turned, we linked, and then he came out and ran back toward me as I ran backward, stopped, and then rubbed and rewarded him.

We moved together in harmony, we ran together, we cantered simultaneously, side-by-side. As we cantered, I held onto his mane, matching his rhythm, then jumping just ahead of his cantering motion, which gave me a boost as I sprang into the air and onto his back as he continued moving forward.

"What an awesome feeling of harmony that was," I said as we continued to watch the scene unfold in front of us.

We cantered along, and then did a few flying lead changes and turns, bareback and bridle-less. The best bits were when we stopped together and I stood up on his back while he relaxed and ate grass.

"As I waved to the crowd of people watching, I remember thinking to myself, *that friendly game has come a long way*," I said to Peacemaker, watching as I saw myself slip off Sharka's back as the music ramped up. I asked him to bow, which he did perfectly. I stood and accepted my applause. "What struck me more than the audience response was the approval of Sharka," I explained, as Sharka turned his head and almost seemed to say, *well done*, like he was pleased with me. "What a fabulous gift he shared with me."

We were suddenly whizzed out of the scene. Peacemaker smiled, looking pleased with me.

"This is major progress," I said. "I feel incredibly proud to have reached this pinnacle of relationship with Sharka, who mirrored my changes and enabled us to both make a huge turnaround."

"Yes, you both were glowing with the transformation of reaching this place together."

"Yahoo!"

"Then you had to leave him again to go back to the states?"

"Yes, I did. It was gut wrenching to leave him. Three things enabled me to do that. First, I felt completely great

about the dreams and things we had achieved together. He was also 17 years old. And finally, I just knew I had to go back and learn some more."

"And you knew that if you stayed in this place, you would not grow again or move to the next levels that you wanted?"

"Yes," I replied as my necklace started to glow. But this time, the change in the necklace was different, a pulsing. "This is unusual. Let's have a look…"

On a Saturday morning at the beginning of a U.S. Parelli tour stop, I handed Pat and Linda their shiny and magnificent horses. The background music stopped while the spokesman introduced the morning's schedule.

"Welcome everybody and let's put our hands together for Pat and Linda Parelli!"

The audience cheered as Pat and Linda ran into the arena with their horses and let them loose. As the loudspeakers pumped out a catchy tune, everyone's excitement built as they sat on the edges of their seats waiting for the pieces of wonder and inspiration that Pat and Linda would display and discuss.

I was proud of the fabulous way the horses looked after my grooming as I watched them under the lights, their coats glistening as Pat and Linda moved them around the arena. The horses showed huge exuberance and character as they interacted with each other. I watched intently, loving this piece of the show.

The crowd went wild as the horses circled in different directions. Then Pat and Linda caught their horses' attention and invited them in. The horses responded enthusiastically and ran to them. Then Pat and Linda put halters on the horses and started to show different pieces of their horsemanship.

Enchanted Glasses

As the music changed to another upbeat tune, I grabbed a barrel to sit on and watched on the sidelines with a couple of other teammates as the demonstration continued. One of the perks of grooming on tour was the privilege of watching the demonstration every week. I was the envy of a lot of people.

Meanwhile, unconscious jealousy ate at my heart like a termite devouring a piece of wood. I wished I was in the spotlight, and I was annoyed that no one had recognized my talent and given me bigger opportunities. Instead, I felt like I wasn't wanted there; there was just no one else prepared to take on my role. The jealousy turned into resentment, which morphed into a feeling of being incredibly knowledgeable and superior in my ability to notice and pick up on all the little mistakes in the performance. I felt good that I could recognize and understand the small details and pull apart the pieces that I could see that Pat and Linda needed to change or improve.

I started to talk to one of the other team members about what the Parellis were not getting technically correct, when the other member made a casual comment that shook my world.

"Well, could you do any better?" she replied.

I felt like I had been punched in the stomach and was fighting to get my breath back. My emotions swirled as the words played over and over in my mind. I realized that I would not be perfect either, and that people could and would pick apart my holes too. Anyone can pull someone and their horsemanship apart; that is incredibly easy and does not take a huge amount of skill. But, could I find all of the things that I really liked and try to emulate them? That realization was a huge BFO

(Blinding Flash of the Obvious). Instead of finding evidence of their mistakes, I could aspire to do all the fantastic and fabulous things that they do.

I felt like a cheat and a jerk for being so critical, especially in the position that I had been given. My huge revelation helped me to completely shift my focus. The jealousy dissipated and turned to belief and hope. I trusted that I could learn and grow again. I changed my attention and could see so many fabulous things that I wanted to emulate. I was excited again and started to watch with much more intention.

The music faded as I found myself back with Peacemaker. "You didn't realize that you were jealous did you?" Peacemaker asked.

"No, that never occurred to me. I thought I was just bitter about it all not being perfect. I didn't see at all that it came out of a hurt place. I just thought that I learned that I needed to see the positive and focus on good things."

"But what you really wanted was to feel loved and accepted and part of the team, and this was your way to feel important to try to placate those bad feelings?"

"Yes, I guess so," I paused reflecting. "Funny, how making that shift and starting to see the positive things they were doing helped me start to love and appreciate other things, even when I was not getting it back. I was so stuck in my stuff. I wanted to be loved and accepted, and I was looking to the wrong places for it all. They accepted me, or I would not have been in that position. They saw the talent and ability in me. I just had to step into that. What you focus on expands."

"So, did you notice the small freckle that I have?" Peacemaker joked, breaking the intensity of the moment.

Enchanted Glasses

"I might have noticed it, but the beauty of the rest of you outshines that," I replied, and we both laughed.

"This is a massive gem for me," I continued. "We have the ability to focus on so many things. It's amazing sometimes what we concentrate on," I wondered aloud as I felt the profoundness of my revelation.

"Like that patch of grass over there. It looks awesome," Peacemaker said distractedly and headed toward the object of his attention.

"Oh, Peacemaker, if only you could stop thinking about your belly!" I responded jokingly.

Whoosh. We were zapped to a new scene.

Inner Beauty and the Brush

The day was hot and dry, sunny with a soft breeze blowing. I was with a group of girls walking up the long incline to the lodge in Pagosa Springs. The climb felt easy, as we chatted about our horses. The anticipation of lunch and a break was a fun change from the morning.

My attention was distracted as I noticed a very cute guy riding a white horse bare back and bridle-less in the round pen. I breathed some deep, soft breaths, enjoying the scene. I watched as he trotted in a soft rhythm, his golden hair bouncing softly in time. I couldn't help but notice his big, strong shoulders through his white shirt. Feeling a little light and excited, I was definitely attracted to this man.

He acknowledged our group with a beautiful, warm smile and a small movement with his finger while he tilted his head forward. The gesture struck a chord in my heart, and a question in my mind. *Could this be my knight in shining armor?* I smiled back, completely in my heart at that moment. I continued chatting with my friends and headed for lunch, the fabulous moment etched in my memory forever.

"Hmmmmm," I said while taking a deep breath as we pulled out of the scene.

"Sounds like you were pretty taken with this handsome young man," Peacemaker observed.

"Oh yes, I was." I hesitated for a moment, a tug at my heart. "Part of me wants to tell you that was an incredible moment, love at first sight. We just knew we were right for each other and it was happily ever after and all that."

"Sounds like a great story, but..." Peacemaker encouraged.

"But, I would be lying... And you would miss out on hearing about some incredible learning experiences I had. I have to thank Don, the handsome horse rider, for so much. He is amazing. But I had to learn and heal a lot before I was ready for a relationship."

"You have piqued my curiosity," Peacemaker commented, and then asked, "So, how did you get to know each other and get ready for a relationship?"

"Well, it started before we even knew each other... with my lists."

"Your lists?"

"Yes, I wrote four lists before I met Don. I don't know if it works in horse land the same, but in my experience you can be attracted to a lot of different people. Now, attraction is incredibly important, but just attraction without other qualities is not a deal maker."

"So how do you know if there is anything more than just attraction?"

"You find out over time. You may have your heart pulled around in the process. However, if you don't have a list and an idea of what you want, then you can enter a relationship with your head in the clouds and hope it

works out and that they are the person you dreamed of. That is quite a risk," I explained.

"Okay, that sounds logical. So, you are writing up a dream board of what your perfect person would be like?"

"Yes, you are right."

"What are the lists?"

"I have four lists. List number one… What I want and need from a partner. For example, he likes horses, wants to live on a farm, likes the outdoors, etcetera," I explained.

"I'm surprised you wanted a horsey guy," Peacemaker joked.

"Oh yes," I replied with a twinkle in my eye and raised eyebrows. Then I continued. "List number two… What I just could not tolerate. Like someone who is an alcoholic, a smoker, or takes drugs, or someone who verbally pulls me down."

"So, no dehydrated-looking people?" he quipped.

I shook my head at my funny friend and replied, "Are you listening to me?"

"Yes, yes. Go on."

"List number three. What I would give to the relationship. This one was tough. I had to think about the qualities I have and would share, and how I could be a great partner someone would want to be with."

"Did you find any?"

"Yes," I replied adamantly, trying not to take offense when I knew that Peacemaker was just trying to be funny.

"Well, please, do share."

"Well, I would be a listening ear, a support, give love no matter what, be committed, loyal, a great friend, someone to have fun with, someone to help challenge him to be better and dig deeper. Get the picture?" I asked.

"Yes. I bet that really helped you to see things in a new light."

"It changed my perspective, thinking about what I could give, not just what I wanted from someone else," I replied.

"I like what you've got so far. What is list number four?"

"List number four is a description of the perfect guy for me, including spirit, as well as looks. I would close my eyes and imagine his presence and how he would feel. That was a really great experience," I said with my eyes closed, feeling a warm glow.

"How did the lists help you in finding a partner?"

"They really helped me stay on track. I would meet someone and they didn't match the qualities on my lists. So even if you are attracted to them physically, you steer clear and don't let yourself get carried away. It's a lot easier than getting involved and finding out later they didn't fit."

"Like shopping and knowing what you want," Peacemaker observed.

"Exactly. So when I met Don, I was excited to find out over time that he met all the things on my lists, and his spirit felt fabulous, really fabulous," I said in a dreamy voice as I took in a deep breath, closing my eyes and feeling Don's spirit and energy and love. I smiled, feeling vulnerable and open. I took in a big sigh."

Peacemaker interrupted, "So, did Don meet everything on your list?"

Not really wanting to pull away from my wonderful moment of feeling my honey, I answered, "Nearly."

"Nearly," Peacemaker repeated. He had a shocked look on his face as he wiggled his head at me inquiringly.

"Okay, everything but his height," I replied.

"His height." Peacemaker had an alrighty-then look on his face.

"Yes. He is six feet, two inches and I had written six feet even."

"Oh, I see that was a deal breaker," Peacemaker joked.

"Ha, ha. Not at all. That was a very negotiable thing. Some things are negotiable and some are not."

"So it was a happy ending for you and Don?"

"Absolutely yes! But, it was quite a road to get there. Let's just say that without him, I would not be the person I am today."

"You two started going out?"

"Yes. In fact, there was something so different about our relationship. I felt like we connected on a spiritual level and of course, were incredibly attracted to each other, too." I smiled at the thought.

"You mean, you…"

"We did not like being separated and at the same time, we were scared of getting too close. There were some small things like age and religion that helped slow us down a lot. There were a couple of things that I did not define on my lists. Mainly, we both had some growing and self-discovery to make before we could come together."

Peacemaker and I continued walking. He said, "It is a blessing that relationships help you to grow and move, one way or another. There are many areas in your life to improve, trying to find and live in that true and authentic place, living where nothing holds you back." He paused, then turned to me and added, "I guess it is a never-ending goal."

"It's a pretty big and idealistic perspective," I replied, thoughtfully digesting his words. "I think it is part of what life here on earth is all about. You are born this perfect little bundle of joy, and as you grow up, through experiences, you tone yourself down and somehow forget to be the beautiful creation you already are. You forget to get out of your own way and let your light shine."

"Yes, I can see that," he acknowledged. Then he declared out of the blue, "I have a surprise for you!"

Before I had a chance to respond, he turned his head to the left and said, "Look."

Following his gaze to an old, wide tree stump, there suddenly appeared a beautiful silver hairbrush. Keeping in mind my quest and unsure of what this surprise was meant to say to me, I simply replied, "Thank you."

"Well, go and look at it!"

As I walked toward the hairbrush, I could see the beautiful detail of flowers and leaves etched in the design on the long handle. I shook my head when I thought I could see a shimmering, like fairy dust, under the brush. That made me curious, and cautious at the same time.

"This is quite beautiful. Thank you Peacemaker," I said, as I picked up the brush and admired it. "So this is a nice way of telling me I need to tidy myself up?" I joked.

"Well, you can tidy yourself up on the outside, but what are you emanating from the inside?" Peacemaker retorted.

"Now you have me thinking," I replied.

"Brush your hair and think of who you are," he proposed.

I reached forward and picked up the brush, which felt lighter in my hand than it looked like it would feel. I brushed my shiny brown hair with long, slow strokes, unsure of how it would help me emanate beauty from the inside. After getting a few tangles out and neatening my hair, I said, "Thanks. That feels better. My hair needed a good brushing." I put the brush back down on the tree stump.

"Wait, here is a mirror." Peacemaker turned his head and looked to his left. Sure enough, as I followed his gaze, there was a mirror in another tree, popping up out of nowhere. *Things seem to do that around here*, I mused to myself.

I looked into the mirror and then said to Peacemaker, "Thanks. That looks better." I was uncertain of what the brush and mirror were really all about, and why I needed them at this stage of my journey.

Encouraging me to go deeper, he said, "Look to your core and try again."

I reached for the brush and picked it up again, looking into my core, but still not getting the point. I started to brush my hair again, asking myself, *I wonder how I am supposed to be? I wonder what true beauty is meant to look like?*

The beautiful brush moved through my hair with ease. "Relax," Peacemaker encouraged.

I didn't realize I was tense until he said something. Lots of thoughts came up in my mind. *How do I need to be, what do I need to be, oh, and now relax.* I was caught in the whirlwind of my mind and getting stuck there.

"Breathe," he encouraged me. I took in some great big breaths and let the air flow out of me, deciding that I couldn't make anything happen, so I would just be me.

Inner Beauty and the Brush

When I looked in the mirror, I was startled to see shimmering white lights sprinkling out from the brush and sparkling in my hair as I moved it, like a wand spreading its love.

"There you go. You are starting to embrace it."

"Embrace what?" I responded, looking at Peacemaker, who motioned me to look back at the mirror. I turned my head and saw a rose in my hair. "Oh, it is beautiful!" I uttered while smiling and taking in more deep, relaxed breaths, which happen naturally when I am my authentic self with no limits. I was beginning to understand what Peacemaker was helping me do.

I closed my eyes and instead of thinking of how I *should* be, I let myself flow, being *who I am*. I inhaled the fresh pine in the forest and asked myself, *Who am I? What is the truth about me and my inner beauty and strength?* I lifted the brush again and ran it through my hair, this time with my eyes closed. A natural smile spread across my face. I felt my inner magnificence and love radiating out of me. Startled by this, I opened my eyes. The feeling was different and almost scared me. I breathed slowly again and this time, closing my eyes, I let that feeling flow, just a little bit.

After a time with my eyes still closed, I felt relaxed and in myself, with no blocks. The feeling of confidence and self-acceptance was strong. I felt like I was starting to glow.

Peacemaker watched me play with this and seemed delighted that I was open to experiment.

I slowly opened my eyes to look in the mirror. The light was coming out of me. I was glowing, not red, but a pure white glow that was bright and beautiful, flowing

from my heart and spreading through my entire body. What I noticed was that, strangely, it took no effort to just be who I truly am.

"Wow," Peacemaker said as he bowed down to me. "You are a real princess." He paused, and then continued. "People will see that radiance that you are putting out. Stand up tall and continue to be and walk in who you are."

"Thank you, Peacemaker," I replied as I enjoyed feeling the bright shiny me. I looked back in the mirror and noticed through the glow that I had a beautiful, dainty princess crown on my head and I was wearing a long cream dress with delightful small purple flowers on it. The fabric was light and trimmed with purple edging. I was emanating the beauty and uniqueness from the inside out.

"You have found glimpses of this often, but you are moving closer to being able to capture and live in this place all the time," Peacemaker observed.

"Yes, I am!"

"Keep the brush. It is yours."

"Thank you." I looked down, wondering what I would do with this fabulous gift. A knapsack appeared, ready to hold my new treasure. I placed the brush carefully inside as I admired the gorgeous dress in the mirror. "The dress is just beautiful," I said, swinging the skirt around so it swayed back and forth. "I love to dress up and look good. It helps me feel better about myself."

"It is even better when you look good from the inside out," Peacemaker replied.

"It sure is."

"It didn't used to be that way did it?"

"No. I had stages in my life where I did not look after my inner or outer appearance. That's because I didn't love and respect myself."

"What shifted?"

"A lot of things. Outwardly, I started to wear nicer clothes and makeup, and do my hair, which showed that I was loving myself more. Consequently, people started to love and accept me more, too."

"That is a great lesson for us all. You have to have self-love and acceptance before you can love and accept others. You can only love others as much as you love yourself," Peacemaker affirmed.

"And inwardly is a whole other story. The truth is, I didn't have a lot of love and self-acceptance of myself. I actually used the horses as an excuse for that. The horse doesn't care what I look like. I just get dirty anyway. No one will be seeing me, so I can just chuck on any old thing and go."

"I see. You are not talking about beauty being what we see in the media and on magazines, are you? You are talking about the inner beauty that comes from within when you have love and self acceptance," Peacemaker stated.

"Yes. When you are feeling that splendor and flow from within, you want to wear nicer things, do your hair, and wear a little makeup to accentuate the beauty that you are radiating. It makes you feel better about yourself. It seems to be a cycle. If I feel better about myself, then I want to wear nicer things and look after myself more. Then I actually feel even better about myself."

"Okay. You've talked about some physical changes. Tell me more about this 'feel better about yourself' thing," Peacemaker suggested.

"Well, I started to feel better about myself when I learned what love, honor, and respect really mean. Strange as that sounds, we have ideas about what things mean. And when you look them up in the dictionary, for example, the meaning is not always the same as our perception of it. So, I did some study on these words for more clarity, using the dictionary and Bible for reference. I found some inconsistencies in my understanding and started to change my awareness of those concepts. This helped me to love, honor, and respect myself, and I started to not only dress better, but to also stand up for myself from the inside, knowing I am worth something, that I am unique, that people like to be around me.

"Another revelation was that I would want to do whatever Don wanted so I could be with him. Nothing wrong with that when you are in love. We all do things to be with someone that we really like. There is a line though. You need to be your own person. If I am tired and need an early night, then I need to respect and love myself enough and get that sleep. That is just one example.

"Having that new understanding was quite freeing in many ways, and it certainly made me feel much better. I was also surprised and amazed at how, with the changes I made for myself, other people started to love, honor, and respect me so much more, too. If I could not do that for myself, then no one else was going to either. Quite an eye opener."

"Well done. Sounds like you really made a shift to loving yourself from within. That causes a significant difference in how everyone treats you, and most important, how you treat yourself," Peacemaker replied thoughtfully. Then he raised his head and his entire body filled with energy.

"Come on. We have some more places that we need to be. Let's get going."

We started to walk again, making our way through some thick woods. As I moved forward deep in thought, I thought I heard someone whispering.

Emotions, Vows and Wows

"Can you hear that?" I asked.

"Hear what?" Peacemaker replied.

"That whispering."

"Maybe you are just hearing the wind blowing through the trees."

We walked a little farther on the path. I heard more whispers and slowed to listen. I began to hear things that I could start to understand. I stopped in my tracks and cocked my head to listen.

"Have you heard about Peacemaker? He is not to be trusted, you know," the whisper said in a low tone.

Not to be trusted? I thought to myself. *What do you mean? He has been very helpful.*

"He is going to get you into trouble."

My brain searched for some truth to the whisper I just heard. *Well, he did nearly get me stuck in a waterfall.*

"He is using you for his own reasons. This is all a ploy, this helping you on a quest."

What if he is using me for his own reasons? I really do not know where we are going, I agreed in my mind. I stopped, shaking my head, wondering to myself, *What is that buzz and crazy thought going on in my mind?*

I jogged to catch up with Peacemaker. "Peacemaker, did you hear all of that?" I asked in a loud voice, as if to drown out the whispers I had heard.

"No. I didn't hear anything."

"I thought you could hear everything that goes on in my mind?"

"Most of the time I can," he replied. He glanced at me out of the corner of his eye, a mixture of curiosity and concern in his look. "Be careful what you listen to," he cautioned.

"How weird," I replied. We continued to walk and a few minutes later, I heard the whispers again.

"He is leading you down the wrong path."

I looked up at the path and saw that there was a fork coming up. An uneasy feeling crept into my stomach.

"Don't follow him. Come this way. Head over here. This way is much better," the whisper said.

As we came to a junction in the path, I started to doubt whether I should follow Peacemaker.

"This is the way," the whisper taunted.

Surprised at the indecision I was having, I thought I saw something move in the shadows. I shook my head as I looked again at the trees. There was nothing there.

Peacemaker is taking me on this quest, and he is leading me the right way. I am sure of it, I argued with my own thoughts and the whispers. I dismissed the chatter and put more energy into walking.

"Come on dawdler. Keep up," Peacemaker teased.

"I'm coming," I replied as I ran to catch up with him, passing the fork in the road. I fell into step behind him again. We walked for some time without speaking, both of us deep in thought.

Finally, my curiosity arose again. "How far do we have to go?" I asked.

"Not too far now. Do you want to ride?" he asked.

"No thanks. I'm fine," I replied, feeling awkward about the dialogue that continued in my head.

We kept walking and then I heard the whisper again. As I saw another fork in the path ahead, the whisper grew louder. "Don't follow him that way. He is taking you on the wrong path. If he turns left, you are in trouble. Stay to the right. He has not told you everything, has he? What about when you had to jump, but he didn't tell you he could fly?"

Oh yeah, I thought to myself. Feeling the distance growing both emotionally and physically between Peacemaker and me, I again began to doubt our relationship and where we were going.

I heard the whisper again. "This is your last chance to get away. Take the other path. For your own safety."

As doubt and confusion filled my mind, a moving shadow caught my eye again. As I focused on it, I could clearly see it was the black horse I had thought I had seen earlier. I followed the outline of the black horse moving through the shadows in the trees. It ran off ahead of us, down the other path. Intrigued and spellbound by this other horse, I started to follow it down the path on the right.

What if I am meant to meet this other horse and I was heading the wrong way? What if I missed that opportunity? The thought raced in my mind. I had to make a decision.

I ducked down the other path. Seeing the black horse disappearing into the distance, I started running. *Maybe I can catch up with the horse. Maybe he is hiding from Peacemaker.*

Emotions, Vows and Wows

A short distance down the path, I suddenly started to question what I was doing and where I was going. *Why is this horse not showing itself, or waiting for me?* I strained my eyes to try to see where this horse had disappeared.

"This is crazy," I said aloud, although to myself. Peacemaker was not with me. Realizing what a silly decision I had just made, I stopped to turn back toward where I had left him.

Suddenly, my feet went out from under me, as the ground beneath me abruptly vanished.

"I'm falling!" I gasped as I started to drop. I couldn't feel or hold onto anything and panic set in. I felt like I was dropping straight down, but then I hit something, not as hard as I would have expected with the amount of distance I felt I had fallen. Something was underneath me as I began to cascade more quickly down the dark hole. There was no time to be afraid or to think. All I could do was go with the turns, the movement, the jarring bumps on the wild ride I was on. My stomach tried to catch up with the jolts and collisions with the sides of the tunnel I seemed to be moving through.

As I took a wide turn and felt myself on a shallower gradient, my speed slowed. Everything came to a halt as I rolled off the end of whatever I had been sliding on and was dumped unceremoniously onto wherever it was that I came to rest. As abruptly as it started, it stopped.

My eyes struggled to adjust to the dark, but I could not see a thing. I noticed a dank, unpleasant smell. Keeping my head absolutely still, I moved just my eyes, as though moving my head might disturb something in this dark place that I did not want to arouse.

As I began to get my bearings in the dark, the quiet was disturbingly still. I heard a drip. *There must be water*

in here, which explains the damp smell, I thought to myself. I checked myself to see if I had been hurt on the descent. Amazingly, everything worked. I hadn't broken any bones, or even had any cuts or bruises.

I wonder if I should call out. Peacemaker would have picked up that I went another direction. What was I thinking, listening to that voice and following that dark mysterious horse? I wonder if Peacemaker will look for me or if he is upset that I ran down the other path?

"Peacemaker!" I called out, risking being found by the dark horse. The sound of my voice startled and frightened me as it echoed off the walls surrounding me. I waited, but there was no reply. Not hearing Peacemaker's voice and being in this strange new place was disturbing. My brain wasn't engaging. Was the quiet and not knowing what was going to happen to me more frightening, or was it because I didn't know where I was? Then I heard the whisper again.

"Peacemaker is not going to help you out of this one," it taunted.

"Be quiet. I am not even going to listen to your lies," I retorted, the echo rebounding around the underground room I had fallen into. My voice was strong, but on hearing the whisper I had jumped with fright.

At that moment, I remembered my heart necklace. I reached around my neck for it, relieved that it was still there. I held the heart shape in my hands.

"Please light the way with your glow," I whispered. The necklace seemed to embrace me, but did not light up. I was perplexed. *Why doesn't it light up?* I thought to myself.

Then I heard a voice in my mind. "I only light up with a chronicle," it whispered back to me. I sighed with the knowledge that the necklace was still with me, and wondered what on earth I was going to do. I did not want to move around, as it was pitch black. Still sitting down, I buried my head.

"Where are you Peacemaker? What have I done? What is going on?" I whispered into the darkness, which just seemed to get darker as I tumbled into self-pity. "Oh, I really don't like the dark. Aaaaargh!" I called out in anger and disgust at my decision and the situation in which I found myself, coupled with my inability to change anything that was happening to me. The echoes in the darkness scared me to the core. I folded my arms around myself, pulling my knees to my chest for comfort.

"You set me up for this one, Peacemaker," I said quietly, giving some blame to him in an effort to help myself feel better about my situation. "Okay, I give up. I don't want this dream anymore. Let's go home."

I pinched myself to see if I would wake up. Opening my eyes, I saw that it wasn't a dream. "I'm still really here," I said with dejection.

In my mind, I started to hit my head against the wall, even though I dared not move.

"What am I doing?" I said out loud. I looked down to see my necklace start to glow. I grabbed it, clinging to its radiance. Looking around the dark cave, I saw nothing but rock. I looked back into the necklace, and zap, I was in a new scene.

"I thought he was the one," I said, bawling to my friend. "I can't seem to stop crying. It's like someone turned on a tap in me and I can't turn it off."

My friend hugged me tight and replied, "It's okay. I understand you gave your heart, and you feel like it got trampled on and then he gave it back to you."

"That's exactly how it feels," I replied with red eyes, pleased that someone understood the agony of my breakup with Don.

"Maybe you should see a counselor," my friend suggested.

"A counselor?"

My emotions felt like they were on ice and I had just lost control, spinning 360 degrees. My head was screaming with resistance. Counselors are for people with problems, who are crazy. I couldn't imagine that I would or should ever need that for me. But as if in slow motion, I went from the shock of her suggestion to wanting to get angry to a reality check. My head said, *Look at you, you are a mess. What are you going to do without help?*

"Maybe I should," I admitted, with a dazed piece of reality sinking in to my reasoning.

My necklace flashed me away from the scene, saving me from feeling that gut-wrenching pain, and zipping me into a new story.

My counselor, Barb, sat in front of me, holding up one hand. "Name some positive emotions."

"Love, peace, joy, happiness," I replied hesitantly. I was a little uncertain why she was asking me that question.

"Great," Barb replied. Then she asked the big question. "Where do they come from?"

Whew, an easy one, I thought to myself. "God," I replied confidently.

"Yes," she confirmed. Then she held up her other hand and asked, "What are some negative emotions?"

I thought for a moment, and then said, "Hate, anger, frustration. I can't think of any more."

She filled in, "Fear, doubt," while holding up her ring finger, then her pinkie. "Where do these emotions come from?" she calmly asked.

That question really got me thinking. God wouldn't make bad things. "Satan?" I said out loud.

"Satan doesn't create things," she replied, pausing for me to respond.

"God?" I asked, unbelievingly.

"Yes," she responded.

Everything about that conclusion felt wrong. Why would God make something bad, wrong, not okay? What a frustrating and mind-blowing thought.

"It is wrong to have negative emotions, right?" I asked tentatively, feeling incredibly annoyed as my concept of the world was being changed. I felt uneasy with the answers I was discovering.

Without directly answering the question, she continued. Holding up her left hand, she asked, "If I do not express and release these negative emotions because I believe that they are wrong and bad and not to be felt, where can they go?" She turned her hand into a fist and placed it over her heart. "Nowhere," she continued. "If these unexpressed negative emotions form a big stone in your heart, when you experience positive emotions, can you openly receive them?" Now she moved her other open hand with the positive emotions toward her heart. However the fist of negative, unexpressed emotions was in the way. The fingertips could reach the heart, but the illustration was very clear.

"So I have less ability to receive the good emotions if I do not express and release my negative emotions?"

"That's right, and you have 31 years of unexpressed emotions to release."

"Oh my gosh, that's a lot," I replied, dumbfounded with the huge realization that was sinking into my brain.

"Yes, it is." She went on to explain, "These emotions will have to be let loose and grieved so you can feel and receive the love that God has for you. This will be a process, with a lot of sorrow – and forgiving."

As everything we discussed began to settle in my mind, I asked, "So, is it okay to feel and have negative emotions?"

"Yes," came the reply.

"Whew," I sighed.

The necklace pulled me out of the scene. I was consumed by the story and how daunting the task of expressing emotions was. That time in my life opened up a whole new world. Then a smile spread across my face as I remembered just a short week later, when I was back in Pagosa Springs and able to identify a negative emotion myself for the first time.

"I'm feeling frustrated." I smiled and named the emotion and felt good about having and expressing it. I found that when I did that, I was not as upset as I had been before, like that emotion lost some of its intensity. Reminded about seeing things differently in my life, I remembered the glasses in my knapsack. I reached in and found them. As I pulled them out, I felt my heart drop with disappointment. They were broken, probably by the fall and slide down into the earth.

As if on cue, my necklace flashed again.

The light of day was breaking on a cool Colorado morning. There is nothing like being up before everyone else and the hustle and bustle of the morning begins. My breathing was deep and rhythmic and my fitness at a peak level as I negotiated the oak brush and ran along the uneven terrain, loving being alone and peaceful in the private wood where I ran every morning. This time is my thinking and praying time, which I cherish.

As I prayed, I suddenly felt overwhelmed. I had been experiencing varying degrees of emotions over the preceding weeks. Kneeling down right where I stood, I let the floodgates open, asking God to help me mourn this stonewall of emotions out of my heart. I sobbed and sobbed, grieving as I felt led. It felt deep and desolate, but freeing at the same time; good in an unusual way, letting it all out and crying out loud, as there was no one around who could hear me.

The feeling of releasing was strange in its relief at the same time it felt huge. I wondered if I was going to be doing this every day for the rest of my life. It seemed as if it was never going to stop. After about 20 minutes, it was as though the door to my heart shut for the day, and I was able to get up and run again, letting the cool air dry the tears. I ran hard with all the energy I had built up inside.

Running always seems to help release the pent up emotion, along with the pain. Luckily, as I ran I had a wonderful thought to hold onto that God had given me: *In one year's time, you will find it hard to believe that you were here. Your life will be so totally and completely different.* I focused on these words as I continued running along the trail.

As I rounded a corner for home, I could see people starting to move about. The release of endorphins and the great feeling of purging the emotions I had been bottling up restored a feeling of peace, giving me a positive place to start the rest of my day.

I descended suddenly from the scene, the dark of the cave blinding in its depth. I sighed. That was a deep and wonderful experience, hard and good at the same time. Remembering the change of feeling that I experienced really gave me some solace as I sat in the dark hole.

Then I recalled another morning that I was out running and praying. After I had returned from that run, I realized that I hadn't gone to that deep and grieving place. I was shocked and surprised, but at the same time it felt right. Like the stone had been removed from my heart.

That was a tough, but great life-changing experience. I learned to face, feel, and express my emotions as they happen, instead of storing them up for later.

My necklace lit up again, enabling me to see more of where I was. I glanced around quickly, and then felt relief for the distraction that would take my attention off of my circumstances. I was back with Barb having another session.

"You have made some limiting vows," Barb explained.

Feeling anxious, I blurted out, "I made vows? Why did I do that? How did I do that?" Stopping to think for a moment, I asked, "What is a vow, exactly?"

"A vow is a statement you make declaring something that you are or are not going to do. They are fairly easy to make, and sometimes we do that very carelessly," she explained.

"I can see that I could have easily made some vows."

"That's okay, everyone does. Let's ask God to show you what they are." She guided me through prayer and God took me back to the scene of my parents fighting when I was a small child. "Okay, what did you say, externally or internally?" Barb asked.

The answers popped into my head. "First, I am never getting married. Second, I am never having kids. Third, I will never put myself in this situation." As the words came out, I was shocked. But they also resonated with me.

"This is true. I have repeated those phrases to many people throughout my life. How could I make those vows at such a young age?"

"It came out of your hurt and your lack," she explained.

"I didn't even realize what I was doing at that young, tender age, apart from the fact that I did not like what was going on between my parents," I said.

"These vows have played out in your life," Barb enlightened me. "You said them for protection, but they are part of the reason that you are here. They have also hindered you from having and enjoying a long-lasting relationship and the possibility of having a family." Barb paused to let all the information sink in.

"I can see how that has been playing out in my life. What a paradox. Part of me really wants a relationship and part of me doesn't," I said, thinking out loud as I started to grasp the meaning of what I had been creating in my life.

Gently guiding me forward, Barb said, "Now we need to break those vows and ask for God's ever flowing and loving forgiveness, so you will not be affected by them anymore and you can move forward."

"Let's do it," I agreed.

As the necklace flashed me back to the dark cave, the feeling of freedom that I felt from releasing those vows

from my life stayed with me. I remembered the changes that came when those blocks cleared, and that feeling of nothing holding me back that replaced them. I felt open and free to choose my own path.

With that thought, I suddenly remembered Peacemaker's last gift. I reached into my knapsack and grabbed my brush. "Even in this dark, I know who I am."

As I said those words out loud, even as they echoed in the dark, I started to believe in myself. As I ran the brush through my hair, a small white glow began to shine from within me. Giving me confidence, I ran the brush through my hair again, standing up and declaring, "I believe!"

My voice echoed through the cave and the bright white light started to emanate from me with brilliant radiance, lighting up the dark around me.

"Thank you Peacemaker," I said quietly to myself.

Although he wasn't there, I felt as if he was saying, "It is all you, not me."

Looking around in the dazzling light, I could see three large tunnels feeding into the space I was in. *Which one do I take?* The decision seemed overwhelming, and then a deep disillusionment overtook me. I would have thought being able to see was positive, but now that I had to choose my path, I couldn't decide.

As I questioned my ability to choose correctly, the glow began to recede and soon I could barely see. Disheartening me even more, the doubt settled even deeper, causing the light to extinguish completely. In the harsh blackness, I realized what I had done.

Standing up, I rummaged in my knapsack for my brush again. "I know who I am," I said with conviction. "I am Rachel from the land of anything is possible, and I am going to take a path, any path, because all paths go somewhere. If it is the wrong path, I can come back and take another."

Taking the brush again, I ran it through my hair and this time, the intense light was almost blinding as my eyes struggled to adjust from the dark to bright light again. I marched forward and took a closer look at the three tunnels.

One tunnel had a lot of cobwebs and didn't look enticing at all. Another had standing water, with moss growing around the edges. The final one had steps.

That looks good, I thought logically. I needed to go back up to where I fell.

I chose to start climbing up the steps of the third tunnel, encouraging myself by repeating, "I live where nothing holds me back. I live where nothing holds me back…"

The tunnel sloped up for awhile, and then started twisting and turning. Eventually it straightened for a very long time, and then more turns, up some stairs, then down. I started to worry that I was going down again, but kept pressing forward.

Suddenly, I heard what sounded like the clip clop of hooves in the distance.

"Peacemaker?" I called out into the tunnel. I heard what sounded like a whinny.

I started to run, and rounding a corner, there he was coming to find me. I ran to him and gave him a great big hug.

Relieved to see me, Peacemaker wiggled with delight as I hugged him.

"Hey there, your glowing-ness. Well done to find your inner beauty to light up the way," he congratulated me.

"Thanks to you and the lessons you gave me. It is soooo good to see you. I am so sorry I doubted you," I gushed.

"You doubted me?" he asked.

"Yes. There was this whispering in my head about you using me for your own reasons, that you have an ulterior plan," I explained.

"Really?"

"You didn't know anything about that, did you? Where did the whispers come from then? Why are there lies running around out there?" I asked.

"There are always lies running around out there. It is not always easy to hear the truth," he replied.

"Well, I did listen to them. I saw a black horse in the shadows and tried to follow him. But he just disappeared off into the distance. Now I feel so bad about it. Will you forgive me?"

"Of course I do," he replied. "Now it's time to get out of here."

"How far is it?" I asked.

"Not too far. Jump on." He dropped down on one leg so I could climb up easily. The roof of the tunnel was higher here and I was able to sit up on his back. Peacemaker picked up a fast walk, and then began to trot through the tunnel. We rounded a few corners, and then I finally saw the light at the end of the tunnel.

As Peacemaker cantered out into daylight, I sighed, reveling in the sunlight and fresh air.

"Look at you," Peacemaker marveled.

Emotions, Vows and Wows

I looked down and saw that my beautiful dress and I were covered in dirt and black marks from our excursion.

"We will have to fix that," Peacemaker said, and then flicked his tail up around me on each side. As he did this, the dirt and marks all seemed to fall off and I looked brand new again.

"Wow, thanks!"

"You are most welcome."

As we continued to walk, I asked Peacemaker, "How do you not listen to the lies?"

"Immerse yourself in the truth. When you are feeding yourself with truth, the lies have no bearing. Take everything into consideration and weigh them all. Meditate on them. Pray about them. Then feel if what you are experiencing resonates with your spirit. Then you will know what is true for you."

"Thank you Peacemaker. I will remember that in the future." I felt incredibly silly that I listened to the lies and followed that black horse in the first place.

Just then, my necklace took us to another scene.

I re-read the paragraph with hope and expectation to ensure I was getting the right information: "Within two weeks you will see a huge change in your life if you follow these instructions. Write down the phrase 'Men love and care for me'. Then below that phrase, write down the first thing that comes to mind. Do it until you run out of thoughts. Do the exercise every day for two weeks."

I paused. *Right, let's do it,* I said to myself. I was a little skeptical about doing the exercise, but was open to give anything a try. I picked up my pen and wrote, "Men love and care for me."

My internal dialogue was ready, coming back with, "Yeah right. Only if they want something." I wrote that down. Then I did it again. "Men love and care for me." Like clockwork, my inner dialogue came up with something else. "So they can get a bit of you know what."

I was shocked at first with what was coming up, but I continued with the process. My brain was very clever and gave me something new most of the time. I could see I was releasing blueprints, thinking patterns, and some surprising programs that I had been operating on for years.

Then it started to change. My brain started to give me different answers. I wrote, "Men love and care for me." This time, my reply was, "My dad does." My next reply was, "My brother does. They want the best for me." I continued to write. "Wow. There are good men out there. There is hope."

I felt my perspective shift, helping heal my heart from the negative wounds I had been holding onto for years.

The necklace plucked us out of the scene.

"Well done. So what happened next?" Peacemaker inquired.

"I wrote that phrase dozens of times over the next two weeks until the replies from my inner voice became more and more positive. They felt more real and true in my heart. I was healing, changing perspectives, and asking God to send the right person into my life. I was now ready and open to receive that person.

"Two weeks later, I received a phone call from a close male friend from the States whom I had not heard from in a long time. We had a great chat. It was wonderful to catch up. This guy is an absolute sweetheart and we were close friends. I felt that somehow the process I had used had released me and I was now sending out congruent waves that I was ready for a partner. My friend called back a few days later and offered me a courtship pledge, suggesting that he come down to New Zealand to spend some time with me.

"I was stunned and flattered, and excited, thinking 'Okay God, it worked. Just two weeks and this must be the guy you had in mind for me.'

"He wasn't what I was expecting, as we had just been great friends, but I was open to the idea. I just had to let Don know, as I had not yet fully let the idea of being without him go.

"When Don heard of the courtship pledge, then the thought of possibly losing me, he was shocked. I was a bit confused, but I didn't realize what God was speaking into Don's life more than 3,000 miles away. He asked if he could come down to New Zealand, too. So, I went from nothing happening to two guys wanting to be with me, all in two weeks time"

"What a wonderful dilemma," Peacemaker interjected.

"Yes, but I was not sure quite what to do. Thankfully, when my friend heard that Don wanted to come down, he graciously backed out, saying that if I was still open to Don, then I had not closed the door there and I needed to pursue that."

"What a strong and graceful guy," Peacemaker commented.

"Yes, he was amazing. I am ever thankful for him being so open and so clear. Okay, God. You have a strange way of doing things, but thank you."

"Quite a turn of events," Peacemaker mused.

"Through all this healing that I did on myself, it enabled me to receive blessings. Now Don had no blocks from my end, and full of ambition and desire he flew way out of his comfort zone over land and sea to New Zealand to be with the one he loves."

"When a man flies across an ocean for you, jumps past his fears and doubts, and pledges his life to you, it is pretty impressive," Peacemaker observed.

"When he lets you know that he would climb a mountain, fight in a battle, do whatever it takes to keep us together, well, yes, that is inspiring. The man that I replied 'yes' to in that magical moment of pledging a promise of being together forever was the man I had already fallen in love with. Although we had already fallen for each other, we were now ready to rise up in love and build a future together."

My necklace twirled us into a new scene.

As I let go of my dad's arm and stepped up beside Don, I felt the connection between us, an indescribable link as our spirits entwined. The presence of God was strong as he wrapped his love around us with incredible peace and overwhelming joy. The church, with its tall leaded windows framed by grey stonework and magnificent beams, seemed to capture and emanate the strength of the beauty and love between us.

The joy and delight that I felt soared in the blessed church in which we held the ceremony. The light cascaded through the windows, uplifting and embracing the spirits within.

I was wearing a beautiful, flowing white gown that gave me a magical sense of being a beautiful and loved princess. I was living my fairy tale, confirmed by the crown on my head.

Emotions, Vows and Wows

Don's eyes filled with tears, and I could feel him soaking in the beauty of our union. My feelings of elation and happiness radiated love from the inside out.

As we celebrated our love, the words "I do" seemed to bounce around the room and imprint on our hearts as we gazed into the windows of each other's souls. The impression of these words, which for both of us mean forever and for all eternity, was sealed when Don took me in his arms and gave me a loving and zeal-filled kiss. Then the fantastic, but strange words, "I now pronounce you Man and Wife" tickled my ears and sent a new smile to my face as we turned around to face the smiling faces of family and friends.

I felt incredibly blessed to be sharing that precious time with the people we love. We proudly walked down the aisle while the church bells rang out declaring the love and union that had just taken place. Everyone was smiling. What a happy and uniting occasion, a precious moment as we both gave and received the precious gift of eternal love for each other.

Swirling out of that beautiful moment, I thanked God for the miracle of how we came together. The incredible love at our wedding healed so much.

"Tell me about that," Peacemaker broke into my reverie.

Startled, I laughed as I said, "I don't think I will ever get used to you reading my thoughts anytime soon." In answer to his request, I continued. "Our wedding had a little bit of, let's say, apprehension for me."

"Apprehension?" he repeated, quizzically.

"The tension between my parents was still pretty high, even after all those years. Having both of my

parents in the same room was stressful. I had not seen them together in a positive way."

"Never?"

"Not that I can remember. So I was not sure what was going to happen. My dad had joked when I was younger that if I were ever going to marry, I would need to have two weddings so that each of them could attend one. All jokes aside, that was not going to do.

"So, I made up my mind. One wedding and they would just have to sort it out or not be okay, but I was not going to let that upset my special day. When I broke the news, I was relieved they were both fine with that. Whew!

"I still had churning in my stomach about the whole thing, them being in the same room and everything. To my surprise, there was not the massive raised emotion and upset I had thought might appear between them on our wedding day. In fact, quite the opposite. They were nice to each other. At the reception, Dad actually asked Mum to dance, and they danced together with us. Looking back at the one picture I have of that moment still brings tears to my eyes.

"Our wedding was not only a beautiful thing for Don and me, it was incredibly healing for my family, both for my brother and I seeing Mum and Dad getting on so well, and the rest of my family coming together. I am so thankful God not only blessed our union, but also healed past rifts at the same time, all in the beautiful moments of love shared. What a blessing."

Peacemaker nudged me. "That was a blessed day indeed. So, what did you do next?"

Emotions, Vows and Wows

"After a wonderful honeymoon and a few months in New Zealand, we traveled back to the States to start our life together."

"New life, no horse. What next?"

Hidden Gifts

"You got it. I needed a horse of my own. Don had a friend around the corner who was selling his horse, so he arranged for a two-week trial, dropping off Dream Warrior for me to see if I liked him. I was dreaming of a warm blood dressage horse, but I knew that finding that dream horse takes time and money, two of which we didn't have at that time. But I desperately needed a horse to play with, and I wanted one immediately."

As those last words came out of my mouth, my necklace whisked us to another scene.

Dream Warrior. There he was as we pulled up in the truck, a cute little chestnut Arab with four white socks and a blaze. Great markings. He had something about him that I was immediately attracted to.

He was in the round pen and I asked him to move around a little. As I watched him prance around the enclosure, more scared than assured. I liked his spunk and the presence in him.

When he cantered, it looked like a deer, four beats, stiff-legged, and leaning like a motorbike. Then he did a slower trot move before stopping, and lifted his leg a little higher. There was an elevated trot step in there that inspired me. I liked this horse.

"Did you see that?" I asked Don.

"Yes," Don replied. "He has some movement in there."

Satisfied with what I had seen, and knowing that I could help out his posture and movement, I said, "I'm going to see what he does if I give him some time to get curious."

"Okay," said Don as he turned off the video camera he was holding to take footage of the possible new horse.

Dream Warrior looked a little scared, so I sat down in the middle of the fairly small round pen to see how long it would take Dream Warrior to become curious and come over and sniff me, or whatever he might do. I looked at my watch so I had an idea of timing. Don walked over and started to play with his horse, Legacy.

Sure that a very long time had passed, I looked at my watch, stunned that only five minutes had gone by. Dream Warrior was still looking out of the pen, not interested in anything that I was doing. I breathed in a deep breath to make sure I was not giving out too much energy that would stop him from relaxing. I took my gaze away from Dream Warrior and watched Don play, which was a good thing, as Dream Warrior did not look like he was relaxing or becoming curious any time soon.

Fifteen minutes later, Dream Warrior interrupted my gaze on Don by putting his head down to eat grass. It took him twenty minutes to even think about eating. I really wanted to see if he would come over. So, I sighed and watched Don some more before finally giving up at thirty-five minutes after Don had finished playing.

Dream Warrior was not even slightly interested in coming over to check me out.

"He is going to need some taming and time," I told Don.

"Yes, he is," he agreed.

The necklace brought us back to the path Peacemaker and I were on.

"Well, what beginnings!"

"Good thing you decided that he was worth taming."

"Yes, it is. He is so worth the time and energy that I put into him. For sure. It didn't take me long to decide that I liked him enough. I really needed a horse, as I had had too long playing with different horses. I needed one horse to play consistently with so I could take him further and do some more advanced things. So we bought him."

"Yahoo, the relationship begins."

"He was a little stilted in his movement, and upside down in his posture, but I knew that I could help him with that. He made some pretty quick changes, and he is a very quick learner."

My necklace rushed us to another place.

There is nothing like the fresh, clean smell in New Zealand after a rainfall. I was breathing it deeply into my lungs, loving it. I was on an early morning run with Jake, my dad and his wife, Denise's German Shepherd, through the rainforest-like bush on the track below my dad's place. The bush is filled with ferns and T-tree, which is just gorgeous to experience while running on the gravel-covered, winding track.

We had arrived in New Zealand three days earlier for Christmas and a holiday. I was so thrilled to be getting some exercise during the holiday, on a familiar track. I had three main goals for this time in New Zealand: family, exercise, and rest.

I felt fabulous, with my breathing free and easy. Jake and I flew down the gravel bush track, down a lot of stairs, and over tree roots and bridges that cross the stream we followed as it wound its way to the sea. We stopped for a moment when we reached the shore.

The green/blue water lapped at the edges of the rocks as we listened to the rhythmic, soothing crash of the waves rolling over the shoreline. So much incredible stimulus. The Pohutakawa trees gently waved in the breeze. A native of New Zealand, the trees were in full bloom with their bright red flowers, reminding me of a Christmas tree.

"Come on, Jake," I called to the dog as I turned. He followed enthusiastically as we tore back up the track. My favorite part on the way back is to go fast up the hills, then slow down on the other side and enjoy the rolling up and down pace. The moisture in some of New Zealand's bush tracks makes it fairly damp under foot, and the short wooden bridges have chicken wire on the middle to keep you from slipping on the green moss that forms. But I had run this track many times before, and felt confident in my steps.

Jake and I tore up another short hill, and started slowing as it dropped down the other side. The track was carved onto the side of a bank, which went up about 12 feet and the same below. There was a little bridge to help you across where the path had fallen away.

As we crossed the bridge with speed, my left foot caught in the chicken wire while my heel slipped on the uncovered moss beside it. The next thing I knew, I was

down the bank on the side of the ravine, glad I had not fallen further down into the stream below.

After taking a few seconds to orient myself, I looked down at my left leg. It didn't look right. Then I looked up the bank and saw Jake whining and pacing, worried as he looked down at me. Jake and the bridge looked a long way up, but I knew I needed to get to the top. I scooted up backward with my arms and right leg, while my left leg literally dangled, a useless appendage.

Relieved to be to the top, I started breathing deeply with the realization of what had happened starting to sink in. *How am I going to get home?* While feeing a dull ache in my leg I began to wonder.

I stood up on one leg to see what I could do. Instantly, a fog of dizziness enveloped me. I quickly sat back down. *Wow, that does not feel good.* Breathing deeply into my chest just made me feel more lightheaded. I settled down, and then tried again. "No, that is not going to work," I said aloud as I laid down while the world spun around me. The reality of what was happening started to sink in. I was in shorts and a light top. Although it was summer in New Zealand, they are very damp. Just as I had been running, I had been collecting dew from the leaves. The mosquitoes were starting to bite. I knew that no one at home would be missing me for a long time, as I run often and am frequently gone for stretches of time.

Jake! I suddenly thought to myself. *What if he runs home and gets someone? That would work!* I took his leash off. If there was ever a time when Lassie was necessary, this was it. "Go home, Jake," I commanded. He ran a short distance, then came back and licked my face. He really had no idea what I meant, and didn't want to leave me. *Great,* I thought to myself, shaking my head.

Trying a different tactic, I thought, *Okay, if telepathy works, now is the time. I need you guys to come and look for me.*

At that point, if I didn't move soon, I was going to get cold. "Alright," I said out loud, mustering up the courage. "I need to get moving. I have to start heading home."

Fighting the dizzy feeling, I stood up a third time, hopping over to lean against a tree and catch my breath. Jake, realizing he was not on his leash, found some interesting scents to explore, then came back to me.

I started down the path, hopping on my good leg from tree to tree. I finally reached one of the bridges I needed to cross, this helping my momentum, as it had railing on each side. I swung my body and landed, then reached forward to swing again. A few swings and I was over the bridge.

That was great, but much too short, I thought to myself as I hopped to another tree, feeling each impact on my injured leg. I continued to hop and swing my way along the bottom of the track until I reached the base of the stairs.

I looked up and took a deep breath. "This will be interesting," I said under my breath. The steep steps were carved into the side of the hill, with wood supports and gravel on top. There were 117 of them to reach the top. I had counted them many times as I had run up and down them in the past. It was quite a hike with two healthy legs. It seemed impossibly daunting with one injured.

I can't hop up those steps, I thought to myself. Instead, I sat on the bottom step and using my arms and one leg,

moved up backward, one step at a time. Logically, it made sense. However, that position sent a shooting pain up my leg. So, forward it was.

Placing the knee of my broken leg on the thin wooden edge of the step, I used my good leg and my arms to pull me up each step. My knee started feeling sore, and looking down, I noticed that it was red with the imprints from the gravel on the steps. The resulting pain caused me to have to wipe the gravel off at each step before putting my knee down.

I went for it up those stairs, my pace steady. At the top, I breathed out a big sigh of relief. I was worn out.

"Come on guys," I said under my breath. *Surely they must be worried about me by now*, I thought.

Hopping over to the fence surrounding a house I started to move to the road. It wasn't easy to hold on to. Reaching the road, I was relieved to see Don and Dad on their way to look for me. My energy seemed to drain away from my body as I waited for them.

"What happened?" my dad asked, a concerned look on his face.

As they both looked down at my leg, nothing needed to be said. However, as they each took an arm to help me hop and swing back to the house, I told them the story of what had happened.

My adrenaline started to wear off, and I began to feel severe pain in my leg. Getting into the car was not working, and after trying a few positions, I said, "No way. I need an ambulance." Denise was on the phone in seconds and the ambulance was on its way. Dad got a stool for me to sit on and Don wrapped a blanket around me, holding my hand and supporting me as I rocked myself, trying to manage the pain.

Hidden Gifts

The ambulance arrived in a short time. Hearing their doors slam seemed extremely loud in my hyper-aware state. Then, in a loud voice, the woman paramedic greeted me, "Hello. Have a bit of trouble today did we? Let's take a look at that."

Their teamwork was excellent as they carried the equipment they needed in from the ambulance. "So what happened to you?" she asked boldly and with certainty.

As I relayed the story to her, she put a needle in my arm and injected a painkiller. "Okay, now we are going to have to cut that shoe off of you," she instructed as she reached for the scissors.

"Those are my new running shoes! I can pull it off," I exclaimed.

"I'm sorry honey, but this is what we are going to do. I would rather get you a new pair of shoes and save your leg right now," she stated firmly. Who was I to argue with that and her assertive manner. They cut my new running shoe off, and not long after that the natural adrenaline and endorphins that had kept the pain at bay started to wear off. Within moments, the pain was increasing significantly.

"Arraaagh. Oh my gosh, it is hurting. Oh, Oh!"

"Here you go, dear," the paramedic said as she grabbed a big tube of morphine, then another and pumped them into my arm. With the combination of adrenaline from the run and getting myself back home, I was definitely high.

"You should start to feel drowsy with the morphine," she explained. But I felt wide-awake – and great, as the painkiller began to kick in.

Suddenly, Peacemaker and I were whooshed to another scene.

I was at the hospital, where they put me under and reset my foot and leg bones back in the joint. I woke up just as I was being taken to a room to rest. The doctors came by and explained that I would need an operation to fix up a few broken bones in my ankle joint and fibula. The thought of having surgery was scary, as I really did not care for needles or hospitals.

"Wow, was I in good hands!" I exclaimed to Peacemaker as I stood watching the scene in front of me. "Although I was frightened about being in a hospital, they are really handy when you need it."

"Yes, they are," agreed Peacemaker.

"The operation happened a few days before Christmas and I was out of the hospital Christmas Eve, just in time to celebrate the holiday with my family," I explained. "Two of the three things that I wanted to focus on happened. I was able to spend lots of time with family, and I got lots of rest! Our time flew by and we headed back to the States two and a half weeks after the operation."

"Were you excited to be back and see Dream Warrior?"

"Oh yes!" I replied enthusiastically as my necklace whisked us to a new scene.

Mid-morning on a damp winter day in Ocala, Florida, Don and I were wrapped up in our coats against the chill. My leg was propped up, sticking out of the front of a golf cart, resting on a pillow. I was delighted to see Dream Warrior, who had become affectionately known as Dreamy, as I spotted him in the herd of about 20 horses. Don opened and closed the gate for us, then we whizzed along the field to say hello to the horses.

Dreamy heard my voice, and looking up became curious. Apprehensive about approaching the golf cart, he finally moved close enough to stretch out his neck and nose and softly wiggle a treat out of my hand. Although he was not interested in getting any closer, I was ecstatic just to be outside with the horses.

Back from the scene, Peacemaker asked, "So what did you do?"

"A broken leg didn't stop me from wanting to play with my horse. In fact, it just made me incredibly distressed. I just had to work out how I was going to do it. I watched some inspirational videos of people permanently in wheelchairs working with horses, and was incredibly impressed with what they could achieve. It was amazing how they could still play with horses with excellence.

"I did not have a wheelchair, but we did have golf carts. They are beautiful, battery-powered legs when yours aren't working that well," I explained.

"Alright, now that's the spirit. So, how did playing with your horse from a golf cart work?" Peacemaker inquired.

The necklace's excellent timing interrupted with the perfect scene.

I angled the golf cart sideways to Dreamy and asked him to come to me. He hesitated, unsure of the cart and not as confident with my stationary approach, from one angle, straight on. That's not the angle that I would normally have approached him. Having never been stuck in one position before, I had not tested or picked up his lack of confidence in that area.

I waited for Dreamy to make a decision, and unlike when I first got him, it did not take a huge amount of

time. He was a lot faster to make a change and try to come toward me. I had to exercise a lot of patience while waiting for him to make a decision. He slowly came over, one step at a time, and let me rub on him. I was relieved that my staying power paid off. I finally got a halter on him. Task number one achieved.

Now we had task number two: Love the golf cart. A quick bit of lateral thinking. Don dropped me off on a cutoff tree stump with a long 45' cowboy rope attached to Dreamy, then had positioned the golf cart 15 feet away from me, straight on. Then I did what I would call trailer loading. But it was golf cart loving instead.

Don kindly positioned a cookie on the edge of the seat on both sides, and left me to it.

I asked Dreamy to move around and get as close as he could to the cart. Initially, he did not even want to look at it, and stopped 15 feet away. I rewarded any curiosity, and then sent him the other way. In no time, he started to get curious and closer to the golf cart.

Watching his expression change as he got closer, then saw a cookie, was great. He liked that idea and reached out with his head and neck and politely picked up the cookie, then moved away again. After repeating this process many times, I was pleased that he started to love the golf cart and head for it. In fact, he started putting his head in it and rubbing on it. I played lots of ground games on it, and soon it became our new best friend.

The necklace flashed to a new golf cart scene.

Some of the truth started to come out. On my own in the golf cart with only a 45' line to communicate to Dreamy, I asked Dreamy to move around. As he was circling me, I watched a little glint in his eye, which piqued my curiosity. Then he turned his head and moved straight away from me, right to a spot that I had no ability to get in a good position to do anything about. All I could do was be bothered by his decision to take that opportunity, while dropping the line and watching him trot off.

He wasn't upset, just very clever. He didn't go that far. He just stopped and ate some grass. I felt like he was saying "na na na na na."

Watching Dreamy figure out that I was not very strong anymore, sitting down with no leverage, was fascinating and frustrating. I realized I had just inadvertently taught my horse where my weak spot was, and I was unable to do anything about it.

After getting over kicking myself, I quickly came up with a plan. I drove the golf cart to a spot where I could pick up the line. I had decided that he was right; I am not strong enough. But the big strong trees just over there are much stronger. I needed to establish in his mind that I am stronger than he is at any angle.

I set myself up for success in a great spot and boldly sent him out again. This time, as the glint in his eye appeared, I took a deep breath and was ready. So was the tree. He went out cantering at the end of the line, and then went to angle off away. The rope wrapped around the tree gave me sure leverage, and I was able to hold Dreamy and the rope firm with the tree's help.

"Yes! A small victory," I exclaimed as Dreamy hit the end of the line, and taken aback, turned and faced me with an expression of surprise. He seemed to say, "Oh, you could hold that!"

We tried again. He is so smart; he got the idea very quickly and became very light and soft on the rope.

Amusing me again with how clever he is, he very quickly got the pattern and started to turn softly before even hitting the line and going the other direction. No more pulling after that pattern, and we were able to drive around all over the place with me leading from the golf cart. He decided that he was very happy to be my partner in this interesting game.

Yet another flash of the necklace, and another scene appeared with Dreamy.

My concentration was intense as my focus was scattered on many things. Dreamy was out in front of Don and me in the golf cart. Two lines were attached to his halter on either side and he seemed to be hooked up to a driving cart. But he was actually only hooked up to me.

I had communicated to Don what I was going to do next so he could maneuver the golf cart in time. I also kept my lines safely in the cart, directing Dreamy to where I wanted him to go. I asked Dreamy to move out straight ahead in the beautiful tree-dotted field, and we moved forward with purpose.

"Okay, I am going to head for that jump over there," I told Don while asking Dreamy to turn and head for the jump. I asked him out to the side a little, while a cool breeze blew on my face. The fence of solid wood with varying heights was spread out in a well laid-out plan in the massive fun playground.

Don drove the cart brilliantly just to the side of the fence so we did not try to tackle the fence ourselves, while Dreamy set himself up and jumped the fence with the perfect footing, then continued with purpose, looking for more. I felt the energy connected to Dreamy as he powered forward, alert and in tune with the surroundings. His ears were forward and his head held high, ready for anything, while still feeling connected to me behind him.

Don helped me negotiate a bridge, and then we rounded a corner and lined up to jump into the trailer. Dreamy jumped in with confidence, as he had done many times before.

"Yahoo! This is fun!"

Like a fast moving series of pictures, we were zipped by the necklace out of the scene.

"So that was like a dream. You break your leg and gain a whole new level of feel without realizing that the gem of learning was there?" Peacemaker asked while walking up to a massive apple tree and finding a beautiful red apple. He bit the fruit as he pulled it off the tree.

"You are right on. It was a huge learning curve. I didn't even comprehend or appreciate how much I used my strength until I could not, or how heavy my feel was until my broken leg made it obvious.

"Feel is not an easy thing to acquire. It has to be learned, and this experience gave me a massive insight to how light feel really needs to be, and how far away I was with my feel."

Peacemaker finished chomping on his apple, and then said, "Oh, these are good." As he reached for another apple, he asked, "Would you like one?"

"I would love one!" I replied as my stomach relayed how hungry it was with a nice, loud gurgle. I hadn't even thought about food. We had been so engrossed in what we had been viewing. I grabbed the apple he offered me out of his teeth and took a juicy, delectable bite.

"There was more than just feel learned in this lesson," Peacemaker continued.

"Hmmmm," I agreed as I finished my mouthful. "Yes, even bigger than feel, I became incredibly thankful for my body, especially my legs and what I can do. It is sad that sometimes it takes losing something to realize how precious it is."

"Yes, I agree," Peacemaker concurred. "These apples are rather delicious," he continued, as we both enjoyed the apples' sweet taste.

I sat down in the shade of the tree. Peacemaker walked over to where I was sitting and laid down beside me. The discussion, then seeing Peacemaker lie down, overwhelmed me.

"Wow, I have been blessed with so many gifts in my life. Watching you lie down reminds me of my experiences of learning. Specifically, asking a horse to lie down."

"What stories do you have about that?" Peacemaker asked.

"Well, the first time I did it, it didn't exactly happen the way I expected," I said, remembering the moment.

"That sounds intriguing. Do tell," he continued, and my necklace lit up. I moved closer to him, and then leaned against his shoulder as the next scene appeared.

I was engrossed in the moment. Sox was a beautiful, athletic, and extremely explosive horse. We were in the middle of a 100 foot round pen with lots of deep sand and room to move. Sox was jumping and twisting, and launching into the air. My concentration was intense, as she did not like the rope hobble that I had around her front leg to hold it up. She was letting me know all about it.

Hidden Gifts

I was holding onto her halter and lead with one hand, and a rope to the hobble with the other hand, which I could release at any moment with a flick of my wrist. But that moment was not the time to do that, since I did not want to reward her explosive behavior.

Sox was a student's horse with a history of bucking. The student decided that she was too much for her and had donated her to the Centre. She was a beautiful chocolate bay with four white socks and a star between her eyes. I so wanted to help this striking horse let go of her opposition reflex and join me in a partnership. What we were working on was what she needed to move forward. She needed to submit her feet, and she didn't agree with or understand the process at all. The intensity of the moment was huge. She showed me some more great acrobatics and exertion. I stayed with her, knowing that I was helping her to come through the other side.

Then she surprised me. She tucked her legs and gently lay down. She looked fine, like she made the decision to stop in that moment. I looked in disbelief, saying under my breath, "What are you doing? That is different."

She stayed there for quite a few moments. I quickly decided to go in and take off the rope holding her leg up, so if she got up quickly the rope would not be in the way. I approached her calmly and patted and rubbed her, then went around behind her, leaning over her back toward her legs to safely take off the ropes. I continued to stroke her, waiting for her to blink and relax. She could have gotten up at any moment, as she was free, but she decided to stay down.

We spent some time just being together. I knew that had made a real difference to her and our relationship.

After some time, it felt right and I asked her to stand up by putting a little bit of energy and rhythm behind her. She got up politely and stood there, very calm and relaxed. We called it a day.

Back with Peacemaker, I continued the story. "I really bonded with that horse. She taught me so much. We did this as a pattern for seven days in a row. She bucked and jumped less and less every day, to the point where she would take one hop forward, but being the resourceful and clever horse that she was, she would choose to lie down in the soft sand. She got a big release from that.

"I would rub her and we would hang out. She got so good at this pattern of lying down, I could lift her leg and ask her, and she would lie down every time.

"But, I felt like it was cheating somehow, because the way she found it was not pretty and I was embarrassed by it. I wanted it to be different," I confessed.

"How did you want it to be different?" Peacemaker asked.

"Lying a horse down should be a romantic fairy tale of huge trust, connection, friendship, and communication. It's on a whole other level. If you teach them to lie down with trust and communication, and…" I hesitated, searching for the right words. "Anyone can force a horse down with ropes, etcetera. I felt like a sham. I had this horse lying down perfectly for me whenever I wanted, but the way she learned it was not how I had envisioned it happening."

"Did she not lie down for you in a relaxed manner with respect and trust?"

"I guess she did, and I received that great gift. I just wish it was not taught from a reactive place."

"How would you want it to happen?"

Hidden Gifts

"What I wanted was to ask a horse to lie down and yield because they can and want to, and they are relaxed and happy doing it."

My necklace sparkled, the reflection shining in our eyes as we moved to the next scene.

The fresh, white snow on the ground caught and reflected the light from the sun, its sparkles twinkling beautifully across the pasture and everything it touched. What wonderful magnificence nature displays. I enjoyed this winter wonderland, tucked up in my snow gear, warm and toasty, while watching my breath extend into the air in front of me.

Seeing me, Dreamy put his ears forward and wandered over with a relaxed, interested expression on his face, putting a smile on mine. Rubbing him and checking that his blanket was straight, I then positioned myself by his side, and by holding just a hand on his mane, I asked Dreamy to walk with me.

He followed my feel softly and we walked through the fresh snow, opened the gate, and walked into our dry covered pen. Since it was so cold, I left his blanket on and positioned him in the middle of the three-sided, open stall and gave him another big rub. He was relaxed.

He looked at me with a peaceful expression and a blinking soft eye. I eagerly bent down and rubbed his leg, picking it up and taking it back slightly, asking him to bow down, which he did, slowly and thoughtfully, without hesitation.

I stood up and rubbed him some more while he continued bowing. I rubbed up around his face and crossed over to his other side, continuing to gently rub him. Dreamy folded his other front leg up and back on

his own, into a kneeling position on his two front legs, very relaxed.

I rubbed his entire body, double-checking that his tail was relaxed. I bent down and reached under him to rub his back legs. I was now ready to ask for the next step. With a little bit of apprehension, I asked him to yield one hind leg, and to my delight, he gently dropped his hind end to the ground and was lying down. I was elated and overjoyed, saying, "Well done!" as I rubbed him some more. He had really thought about it and had decided to yield.

"Good job, honey," Don congratulated me.

"Yes! This is the way it is supposed to be," I replied ecstatically. I rubbed Dreamy some more, and then gave him a treat. I stood back and asked him up. He stood softly.

With a glisten in my eye, I was back with Peacemaker.

"That was a massive achievement. I had dreamed of doing that from the first time I saw a picture of a horse lying down next to a human. I also wanted to teach and ask for this with connection and my horse's consent. It was so wonderful to do it with Dreamy blinking and thinking about it and remaining present," I said, reveling in the memory.

"I bet he appreciated that," Peacemaker commented.

"Yes, I think he did. I have to admit, it wasn't as simple and easy as I might have thought to get there. We did a little bit every day, finishing with something positive and progressive. Sometimes I did doubt if I was ever going to get it this perfect way, but the thought of ropes and all that to help out was not an option."

"I think that is normal in the middle of something, to look for an easier way. But you didn't go there, and that was the main thing," Peacemaker encouraged.

"Thanks," I responded, receiving his compliment. Peacemaker got up and stretched out his front legs.

"Time for us to be moving on. Jump on. We still have a little way to go."

The Invisible Wall

I jumped up on Peacemaker's back and we trotted for a while, and then slowed down, enjoying the sun and the wonderful day.

"What a beautiful meadow. The grass is just perfect, green and not too long. A wonderful length," Peacemaker said as he grabbed a bite while we slowly cruised along at a walk in the open field. I was gently swaying with the rhythm. Happily looking around at the beautiful surroundings, I was taken aback as my eyes caught a dark shadow of a horse in the tree line. The image disappeared as quickly as it appeared.

"Did you see that?"

"The black horse in the shadows?"

"Yes!"

"Let's just ignore him and be on our way," Peacemaker suggested.

Suddenly my face, then chest and arms hit an invisible block. Caught by surprise, my entire body was flat against the wall, stopping me from moving forward. Peacemaker continued to walk straight ahead, unaffected. He continued to walk, his back moving forward with me sliding backward across it, then down his rump, and finally I dropped to the ground in a heap. He stopped and looked back at me.

"What are you doing?"

"What does it look like I'm doing?" I answered sarcastically, startled that I was on the ground and offended that Peacemaker thought I had something to do with not staying on his back.

"Well then, come on."

I stood up and shook myself off, not believing what had just happened. I couldn't explain it. I took a step forward and smacked my forehead and body into an unseen wall.

"Ow!" I rubbed my forehead, then reached out to touch the imperceptible wall. I felt high and low, left and right, expecting to find the edge of the barrier. "What is this?" I asked, stumped as to what was happening.

Standing in front of me, Peacemaker replied, "I don't know. Step aside and let me see if I can walk back through it." He walked toward me, through where I had just felt the wall, as if nothing was there. "It doesn't seem to be stopping me," he observed.

"Great. I am going to try again." Holding my hands out, I walked to the point Peacemaker had just walked through and I was again stopped by the invisible barrier. "Wow, that is so weird. So it is just a Rachel wall," I observed.

"I guess so," Peacemaker concurred as he walked back through it again.

I tried to follow right after him with my arms outstretched, and again hit the hard solid wall. Unbelievable.

"Why can't I go through this and you can?"

"This is very strange. Why, when you have come so far, would you stop now?"

"What do you mean?" I answered, hurt that Peacemaker would blame me, when I was trying, but could clearly not move forward. My necklace flashed. *A distraction*, I thought to myself. *Might as well sit down and watch. I'm not going anywhere anyway.*

The phone was ringing as I stood on a porch on a hot summer day. I reached down and pulled it out of my pocket, reading Lisa's name on the display.

"Hi there."

"Just thinking of you. Had to call and say 'Hi'," Lisa replied.

I was thankful to hear Lisa's voice. We always have great conversations about the deep things going on in our worlds. We've shared so much together over the years, and I feel incredibly comfortable just being me when I'm around her.

"So what's up?" she asked.

"Well, I have to be honest. I'm feeling incredibly de-motivated to play with my horse." I was stunned as the words came out of my mouth and I realized what I had just said. I have never told anyone anything like that before, and it wasn't something that I would just tell anyone. Horses are my passion.

Feeling disturbed, the reality of what I was telling Lisa sunk in. "I just see no reason to do anything. Nothing is drawing me. Yet, I am feeling this incredible turmoil about it," I replied from my heart, feeling the pain lying underneath the layers.

"Well, have you asked your horse what is going on?" she replied without hesitation.

"No," I answered with a bit of surprise, as that thought had not crossed my mind.

"Well, put your hand on your heart, breathe, and ask him."

I took in a deep breath, put my hand on my heart, and looked right off the deck where I was standing and saw Dreamy. I asked, "Why am I so de-motivated?"

After a long pause, I heard Lisa ask through the phone, "Well, what did you get?"

Having been carried away with the moment, the breathing, and stopping to ask the question, I was surprised and relieved by the answer that came. "He says, 'You are not doing what you want to do. You are trying to do what you think others want you to do. You are not following your dreams. You are completing things that you feel like you have already done. That is the wrong focus and it is de-motivating to you. Follow your dreams. Follow your heart.'"

As I heard my own voice relate Dreamy's message, I had another realization. "I have been playing with the Level Four for quite some time. Just recently a new Level Four parameter came out that gives you the ability to actually do something tangible to pass it. I am a bit unenthusiastic about it, as I believe I already am at that level and wish they would just give it to me rather than having to prove it. It is also time intensive. That feels incredibly de-motivating for me," I explained.

"There is more. Keep listening," Lisa suggested.

After a period of silence and listening, I replied, "Oh yes. Wow! I have been trying to do Natural Horsemanship, hoping it will lead me to my dreams, rather than head for my dreams and allow Natural Horsemanship to help me get there."

I breathed a sigh of relief after my realization. I felt like a huge weight was lifted off my shoulders. "I don't need approval from anyone but my horse and my open heart. This feels right, but a whole new level of scary, as now there is no clear path or road map before me. Where do I go now?"

"Ask Dreamy," Lisa reminded me.

"Oh yeah." I took another breath and held my hand on my heart.

"Can you trust me?" Dreamy asked.

"Yes, right now I can," I replied. I felt that place of complete trust and acceptance.

"Okay, let's make some new dreams together. Let's create a road map."

Coming out of the moment and slipping into my logical brain, I felt myself tighten. "What? My own thing? That sounds scary. What if it isn't what I think it is? What if people don't think it is okay?"

"Ask Dreamy," my friend reminded me.

Going back to that place of trust and love, I took another breath and sighed, asking Dreamy what my new future looked like.

"It is beautiful. It is expression and love, and a mixture of everything wonderful. It will be different all of the time," Dreamy responded to my question.

"This is amazing and inspiring. I feel re-energized, and can't wait to get out there with my horse again! Thank you so much Lisa and Dreamy, for being there for me."

"You are most welcome," they replied in unison.

I drifted back as Peacemaker's voice reminded me where I was. "So, you asked your horse?" he prodded me.

"Peacemaker, are you making fun of me?" I responded, feigning a hurt look.

"Just a little," he responded with a mischievous look on his face.

"You are lucky my necklace is glowing again."

Dreamy's hind leg was swollen above the fetlock, putting me into total disarray. My one and only horse was hurt. Luckily, he was not lame. I felt his leg with my hand. It was full of fluid, but not hot. Trying to distract myself, I gave Dreamy a scratch. He felt so good, smelled so good, and had such a wonderful spirit, attentive and willing.

My mind wandered as I thought of the times we had spent together. I had connected with him in ways that I had never been able to with any other horse. In fact, he was the closest example of what I had imagined from the very beginning that a deep connection with a horse would be. His wonderful dark eyes not only looked into my soul, he held my attention with his presence, and was happy to just hang out with me for hours. I loved it when he rested his nose on my head and sat there touching me in the only way horses can without arms, as though he was embracing me fully and wholly as who I am.

He leaned in closer to get a good scratch. I loved it when his nose wiggled with pure delight from the moment, fully receiving the time and love and energy that was being given to him.

My attention came back to his leg. The thought of Dreamy not being okay put me into complete disorder. I was trying not to panic about anything being long term or serious.

Back with Peacemaker, I explained, "As you can imagine, his swollen leg was not a good thing, in so

many ways. Not only could I not ride or play with him, I started to doubt everything that we did together. 'Will he be okay? Will I ever be able to ride again?' I had invested so much into Dreamy in so many ways. I was caught up with doubt and conflict.

"He got a couple of weeks off. During that time, I checked his leg every day to see how it was healing. The swelling went down, but not all the way. It would look okay one day and not so good the next. Time and rest was the best medicine. We were traveling, so another week off would not do any harm."

Peacemaker stared at my necklace, which I didn't notice was glowing, as I was so intent on telling him my story.

I looked at the necklace, but couldn't see anything reflected. "What am I doing, Peacemaker?"

"Sitting in front of a computer watching dressage tests on YouTube."

"Oh yes, there are some really inspiring clips of some great combinations winning modern day dressage. When I watch them, I imagine that I am riding their horse, feeling the power and energy, the lift and the big stride, sitting tall and proud on the horse's back.

"I had also been visualizing riding that test, asking the horse at the right time for each different maneuver, feeling the motion and sensation in my imagination. I knew I was going to ride that some day. But sometimes that just felt miles away from where I actually was at that point. So with not knowing when and if Dreamy and his puffy leg would recover, I felt helpless in moving forward."

"That was certainly a soul searching time for you," Peacemaker observed.

"Sometimes we reach a place in life where we doubt everything. I was full of uncertainty."

At that moment, the necklace engulfed us.

I was chatting with my friend Kelly at her house on the beach in Rhode Island, not sure of anything with my plans for Dreamy. "Dreamy is not naturally talented to do some of the things that I'm asking him to do. It's a stretch for both of us, and I'm putting a lot of pressure on him and myself. I'm in a place where I don't know if I am doing the right thing or not, and that isn't comfortable. In fact, it's a little scary.

"Dressage is like weight lifting. It can put a lot of stress on a horse, and I'm not sure if it is fair to ask that much of him. I have asked him for a great deal, and he has given me a lot. So much more than I could have ever expected. Maybe I should get my new horse, who is naturally talented in the areas that I want to work in, and ease off on Dreamy."

Kelly listened, and as a good friend, agreed that this might be a better way to go.

Back again as I sat on the grass, I commented, "Oh my gosh. It is so easy to take a thought and run with it! Funny how history repeats itself. I remember others saying that about Storm Eagle. 'He is not talented enough.' And here I was doubting and saying to myself the same thing with Dreamy."

"You are taking some huge steps and had some steep learning curves, going to places that you have never been. That makes it uncomfortable for you, and your brain can sometimes think of ways to not have to push forward, keeping you in the place where you are comfortable," Peacemaker observed.

"That is so true," I agreed.

Without warning, the necklace transported us to a new scene.

A few nights later, Don and I were on our own with the sounds of the gentle waves crashing against the shore. I felt Don put me on the spot when he asked me, "Are you really living your dream?"

In the beautiful setting, it was difficult to say anything but yes. However, a tight knot under my sternum told me that wasn't the true answer.

After a pause, I replied, "Yes and no. Yes with family and our life, and everything that we have. But if I were really honest with myself, I would be riding a horse with Olympic potential, feeling their movement." Getting caught up in the thought, I imagined just trotting around on a horse like that. "Even just trotting would be a whole other feeling on a big, striding horse," I said out loud.

"Then we need to bring that horse home for you," my incredibly supportive, amazing husband replied.

With hope, excitement, and a little thrill, I thought, *Yes. I am going to receive this gift. This decision feels really good.*

"That would be cool. I could ease off on Dreamy and not put that same intense pressure on him, at the same time moving closer to my dream with a horse that is naturally talented to do everything required. It would be easier for both of us."

We popped out of the scene.

"Oh Peacemaker, I am incredibly blessed with such a wonderful and supportive husband!"

"Yes, you are," he replied, then became distracted as another scene came into view.

The Invisible Wall

"There is the whole family driving home from our trip," I observed, remembering my heart melting as I saw Dreamy waiting for us.

The horses all watched as we drove up the driveway. "Let's go say hi," Don said. I agreed and we jumped out of the truck to greet the horses. Dreamy looked great.

"It looks like the swelling in his leg has gone down," I observed. I was thrilled, and at the same time felt incredibly bad for Dreamy, like I was cheating on him. *What will he do at the young, vibrant age of 11 if he is not my main flame? Shona, our daughter, is not old enough to take him on as hers yet.* The thoughts pulled at my heartstrings. I didn't feel good about the decision we had made. I tried to tell myself I had time for two, but was that true? My mind was spinning with thoughts.

Life continued moving forward, even when this part of it left me in internal chaos, the doubt filling my mind again. The next few days, I just played a little on the ground to see how Dreamy's leg did with a little ground play. Everything was fine; his leg looked better.

Without warning, my necklace took us to another scene.

I was thrilled to finally be riding Dreamy out on my own on a beautiful day. I felt no pressure at all to do anything special. I hoped his leg looked good when we finished. Being on board Dreamy again felt great. He had lots of energy in his walk, and we were both eager to be out and about. I lifted my energy and Dreamy responded in harmony by moving into a trot. Loving every stride, I leaned forward a little in the saddle as we went up and over little hills, around trees, then up a steep bank to canter around our big track.

It felt good and freeing to be moving and we dashed across the middle of the field. I lined him up for a little jump. I loved that feeling as we jumped in beautiful rhythm. We walked a little more and I took in a deep breath of fresh air, enjoying the gift of this precious moment.

He was warmed up, so I shortened the reins, and with my energy lifted in anticipation, I asked for a trot in a collected frame, just for fun. With the new images in my mind of what the best looked like, the pictures that made me feel like I was miles away, also gave me a great image of where I was going and what it might be like.

There was no one around, just Dreamy and me. A gentle breeze was blowing, with the sun shining and the striking mountains as a backdrop to our ride. It was a spectacular setting.

We did a few transitions to get balanced, and then I collected him, moving him out with some more punch. These small transitions always put a smile on my face, to feel the power of going forward, and then slow and quick.

Then it happened. I asked for a little passage, or elevated trot, and was amazed and delighted, and a little astonished, to feel Dreamy give me some of the best passage that I have ever felt. It was different, elevated and forward, and with power.

Wow! I thought to myself. *It used to feel like a trot in slow motion, up and down and a little bouncy and side to side.* This time was so different. It felt very forward, like we were going somewhere, covering ground, but with lift and extravagant energy. *Knock me down with a feather! Just when I thought of leaving my dreams with Dreamy, I let go of all expectation and everything just flowed with him and from my heart, with a clear picture in my mind, and with me being in the moment. He was giving me more than I ever expected to be able to feel on him.*

I felt like I had just won the Olympics. The feeling was incredible. My whole body was energized, and deep free breaths flowed. I was amazed and excited all at the same time; a great feeling of certainty that Dreamy had the ability within him to do all the things that I wanted to do.

But even with the amazing buzz I felt, there was still doubt and fear in my mind that he might not be a mainstream, competitive horse. Not wanting it to affect the moment, I shook it off and continued to enjoy the ride with a buzz that we both shared as we walked on a loose rein for home.

The feeling of elation stayed with me as we glided out of the scene.

"Peacemaker, that was truly awesome. What a great feeling. It wasn't easy to get there, either," I said.

"But you did it. You nearly gave up, but you held on. Well done!" Peacemaker encouraged me, and then asked, "What did Dreamy teach you with that experience?"

"To trust him and stay in my heart more, and to let it flow. That was a really incredibly uncomfortable thought, as controlling my life has been so much easier for me in the past," I paused, thinking for a moment. "Well, safer, if not easier," I finished.

"Is that safe place a great, open and abundant place?" Peacemaker asked.

I thought for a moment before answering. "No, not always. I guess I do like a bit of flamboyance and change in my life, too. I am learning to live more in that place, and be comfortable and confident there.

"Learning to trust and stay in my heart seems to be a thing that I continue to deal with. Now that Dreamy was sound and moving forward and my questions were changing, there were a few other areas that I needed to address," I explained.

"Like…" Peacemaker prompted me.

"For one, the door was wide open for me to get my Level Four. I had wanted that Level since I started in the Parelli Natural Horsemanship program and heard that only a couple of people had achieved it. The opportunity to get it arrived and I felt cheated that it didn't hold the prestige that it used to hold. Lots of people were passing it, rather than it being a few fabulous people who had it. I was excited that I could actually get it; at the same time, I didn't want to put myself out there on the line again.

"I didn't want to do it, but at the same time, I did. The mental turmoil started. Part of me felt that I should just be given this level without having to prove it. The other part didn't want to go through the emotional journey of being graded by others. I vacillated over that for weeks, and then I decided that I was going to do it. What did I have to lose?

"I went out with no practice and in two days filmed all the necessary categories for my horsemanship. I sent them in. Good enough was good enough. I was just going to see what happened." I paused, as a new realization sunk in to my brain.

"I get it now! I needed to trust." I stood up and walked confidently forward toward the invisible wall, believing that trust was the key to my release. At the last moment, I held my hands up and forward, just in case the wall was still there. Sure enough, they hit the barrier again.

"Arrrgh!" I said as I walked back to the side where Peacemaker was waiting.

"So, back to the Level Four," he said, encouraging me to continue.

"Well, waiting for the results was nerve-racking. I checked the computer every day to see if there was any word. Finally an email arrived. I had passed two sections of my test, which I should have been jumping up and down for joy and celebrating. But there were two left to go and I was bummed that I didn't pass them.

"In my discouragement, I wasn't able to see clearly that the information that came back with the email was not negative at all. In fact, they were impressed with what I had sent them. They said I had showed them Levels Four, Five, and Six, but they just wanted to see some more fundamental things. I had showed a bit too much fancy stuff and left out the clarity of the foundation.

"Now, you would have thought that the end of the world had come. I slumped right back into de-motivation again, as my worst fears hit. I decided that I just didn't want to face rejection again, and that I was not going to re-send in the next two sections. I didn't really need to pass my Level Four anyway. So, I stuck out my jaw in defiance and continued to play with my dressage. One of the sections I *had* passed, and that was my passion anyway," I explained.

Sitting down in the grass, I continued, "Some months passed, and then my own self-pressure started to set in. I tried not to think about it, to dismiss it from my mind. But then the realization hit that I was not setting a very good example for my daughter, and of course to all the students that I was teaching, too. I felt like a hypocrite.

"I have a horse who is Level Four, I am Level Four, and I was letting a small setback and some hurt pride hold me back, stopping me from even trying to move forward. One rejection with encouragement to just show them the basics was causing an I-don't-want-to-do-this-and-I-give-up attitude?

"I realized it was time to stop limiting myself. I had forgotten my mum's advice she would tell me all the time when I was growing up. 'Nothing is impossible.' That's what she used to say. I remembered a quote by Michael Jordan, the famous basketball star. 'I've missed more than 9,000 shots in my career. I've lost almost 300 games. Twenty-six times I've been trusted to take the game winning shot and missed. I've failed over and over and over again in my life. And that is why I succeed.' Michael had a few setbacks, but he didn't let them hold him back." I paused again, thinking about my change of perspective.

"When I was able to change my point of view, the fire was rekindled. I was determined. I changed my attitude, and with clarity, decided that I would do whatever it took to pass this level, even if I had to re-film it 100 times. It's crazy, but after that realization and with this new attitude, I went back and looked at the email. To pass, I only needed to show a few things that were very minor. Again, I went out and filmed without any practice, only with a huge change in attitude.

"I had a clearer picture in my mind of what they wanted to see, and added in the things they asked for. We filmed my Level Four on-line, and sent it in again.

"The filming was easy. In fact, I was able to just go out and do it, like a live audition. I was relieved and excited when I passed my on-line. I was so thrilled. I celebrated my going for it past the fear and pain.

"Next was the section freestyle. I went out and without practice, filmed my freestyle piece. A few weeks later, I had the great news. My freestyle, and therefore my complete Level Four, passed.

"Yahoo! Time to celebrate. After that, I didn't really need to pass for any reason other than Shona and me. That was a great step for me. I learned not to give up, to keep trying, that my mum was right; nothing is impossible. It's easy to feel the rejection and say, 'I don't need recognition' and stay where I was rather than make a decision to do it anyway. I had to change my thoughts and press on.

"Now I know that I can do anything that I put my mind to," I said as I got up off the ground. "Nothing is impossible. I have come this far, I am going to finish," I said as I walked confidently toward the invisible wall, no hands up to protect me from a possible whack on my head, as I finally understood there was nothing that could stop me, apart from my own walls, my own fears, my own limits. "I am going to flow in who I am as a unique being," I said as I continued forward.

Suddenly, there was a shattering sound and I saw thousands of shards of glass-like pieces flying away from me into the air, randomly landing to the side. As I passed through the wall, I turned around and yelled, "Woo hoo!"

"Yes, yes, yes," Peacemaker said as he laughed and gave me a warm nod, as if to say, "You are getting it."

"Thanks," I replied, without even needing to hear any words. "So I made my own wall and I didn't even recognize it," I said, realizing that I have often held

myself back from my own progress before I have even started. "Peacemaker, so many times I've made things bigger and more difficult than they are."

"Yes, and realizing this will help you to recognize when you are letting your own fears and limits stop you."

"That's true. Seeing these things really helps me find a new perspective."

As the words tumbled out of my mouth, my necklace glowed again.

My frustration level was high as I clenched my jaw. I couldn't believe that my flying lead changes weren't clean. My breaths were short, and I felt tense and tight, determined to try again and do it until I got them right. Dreamy was also braced and tight as he reflected my energy, at the same time trying his best to understand and give me what I wanted.

With both our energies high, we walked again in position on our straight line, and then did a nice walk to canter transition to the right. Then I mentally set up and moved my body in an exaggerated way for the flying change skip and then canter to the left. I asked, and got it.

We weren't finished yet. I set up for the flying lead change skip to the right. We repeated that a number of times until we got to the end of our line. The flying lead changes didn't feel good or clean. Dreamy changed to the other lead, but not in perfect timing with hind legs before the front legs.

This had been my frustration for a while, but this time, my brain went somewhere different than before. I listened to my little voice inside my head and actually heard what I was asking myself. *Why can't I do this? What am I doing wrong?*

The Invisible Wall

Surprised by the questions I was thinking, but elated that I had finally realized what I believed, I immediately changed my posture and said, "We can do this."

We went again. But this time was different. I was still focused and determined, but with a softer approach. A smile crossed my face as our flying changes, while not perfect, had improved significantly just with a change in my internal questioning.

My necklace flashed us forward.

After putting Dreamy away, I ran into the house, excited. Seeing Don, I blurted out, "I know what my questions are now!" He listened attentively as I explained. "My questions have been all wrong. How can I find a solution to my problem if I keep asking my brain to answer really bad questions?"

With Don's confused look, I realized I needed to set the scene for him. "I clearly remember an exercise that I did in the Goal Achievement Program that Stephanie Burns runs, called the Labyrinth. One assignment is to see all the things in your world that are the color yellow. At the time, I thought it was simple. There are not many yellow things in my world.

"So I went out the next day, and because I asked my brain to spot yellow, well, spot yellow I did. I saw billboards with yellow, yellow rain jackets, yellow cars. I mean, there was yellow everywhere. I had not been looking for yellow before, and now it was popping up everywhere before my eyes.

"That really helped me understand how our brains work, and how they will try to answer every assignment that we give them. A bit like when you buy a new car or you are looking at a new car and you see hundreds of

them on the road. It's surprising because you believe that you had not seen any, or many, before," I explained.

"So, this is the exciting part. What are the questions I am asking myself when I am trying to get flying lead changes? 'Why can't I do this?' and 'Why am I not doing this well?' and 'Why are you doing it all wrong?' And how about, 'Is your horse good enough?' and on and on.

"Now I have to ask better questions, like…" I paused to think a minute. "'How can I get better flying lead changes? How can I get clean flying lead changes?' Now my brain can find solutions and I'm excited and free to ask other people if I run out of ideas. I feel like I am on my way to solving this puzzle," I sighed in relief. "Now I see a way out; a way forward."

Don replied, "That's awesome. Good job," as we flashed out of the scene.

"Peacemaker, that was an exceptional day of learning. What a gift from God. What a light that went on for me there. I would have been stuck in a rut for a long time if I hadn't changed my questions."

"It didn't take you too long to fix your flying lead changes after that, did it?" he asked.

"No it didn't," I replied, and then added, "And it had nothing to do with flying lead changes. Once I had my brain on my side and working for me, it quickly found solutions to play with. I found out it was the fundamentals that I had to repair to help the end product become beautiful," I explained.

"Seems to me that you heard that a lot… 'The fundamentals.' But it was not an easy concept to understand and really get so you could move to another level," Peacemaker observed, then added, "But when your brain is working for you to answer your good questions, things fall into line a lot more quickly, don't they?"

"Yes they do! That was such an exciting re-discovery and self-learning project. Amazing how sometimes you know something for quite a while, but it doesn't really dawn on you until later," I said as we continued to walk along the trail.

Peacemaker walked a little way, then started moving in an unusual pattern, darting left, then right through the trees, then stopping, backing up, and turning the other direction before moving forward again. I stopped and watched, wondering what he was doing.

"Don't tell me you are looking for treasure," I joked.

Ignoring the jibe, Peacemaker called out, "This way!"

Guilty As Charged

I caught up to him and followed along more closely. After a short walk in and out of more trees, he stopped and held up one front leg. "Stop right here," he directed me. He whinnied, and as I looked around us, our surroundings had turned into a courtroom. I felt the weight of a dark brown cloak on my body, covering me to the ground, swaying with its immense amount of fabric as I turned around.

"Please take the stand. It seems that you have been called into this courtroom," Peacemaker instructed apologetically.

"Take the stand?" I asked, feeling put on the spot. Following his direction, I looked at where he had indicated I go, then tentatively walked over, then up the steps, and sat on the chair. I looked down at Peacemaker, who had donned glasses and a wig, making him look like a cross between a scientist and an English barrister. He looked funny, lightening my surprise and the tension I felt.

His hooves reverberated on the hardwood floor as he moved to his position in front of the jury. At that, I did a double take. *The jury?* There were 30 or so faces sitting and standing on hard wooden bleachers in the jury section, all intently watching Peacemaker. Looking again, I realized that those were not human faces. There were squirrels, deer, mice, raccoons, a few foxes, and a number of chipmunks. As I continued to look at the faces, I saw a dog, a cat, and a horse.

My attention was diverted as the back doors came flying open and the illusive black horse cantered right up to the front of the courtroom in full form.

"Sorry, I am a little late," he said with a deep voice, and with no introductions.

"Order!" commanded the judge, a large moose with a huge rack of horns. With a booming voice, he hit his mallet on the desk and said, "Let's begin. We are here today because the black horse has put on the stand Rachel Jessop for five serious limitations."

"Five limitations? Oh, my limitations," I said very quietly under my breath as I wrinkled my forehead and raised my eyes, thinking of my limitations. Nothing came directly to mind, as all that I could think was *I really don't want to hear this.*

The moose looked to the black horse. "You may begin."

Everyone in the room shifted their attention to the black horse as he began his case. His mocking words seemed to go right through my body.

"Five charges are laid out before you today. Number one: Scarcity. Number two: Un-thankfulness. Number three: Getting Comfortable. Number four: Being Tight and Un-Giving. Number five: Unappreciative and Not Celebrating. It is time to face the music and stand accountable for these limitations."

I gulped. The black horse was now looking straight into my eyes, looking right through them, penetrating my soul and making me feel uncomfortable and vulnerable. I felt a large knot in my chest and a sick feeling in my stomach. My heart was aching.

"Charge number one. Scarcity," he repeated.

My necklace took us to a new scene.

Don casually mentioned in his deep, strong voice that we needed to buy… Before he could finish, I felt a knot in my stomach causing me to almost become nauseous. I knew the feeling too well. It had inhibited my thoughts and movements for a long time. My mind was whirling with backchat. *We can't afford it*, I thought to myself, before he had even finished the sentence. *What about the expenses that we have? We didn't budget for that.* Clichés ran through my head. *Money doesn't grow on trees. It goes out faster than it comes in.* On and on the thoughts continued. I was completely shut down and caught in an old familiar pattern. I didn't like it, but I didn't have any other solutions. My voice was silent, the feeling I was having overwhelming me. I felt stopped in my tracks.

We returned to the courtroom and I felt all eyes on me. I wished I could just disappear or shrink under the stand.

"Thank you necklace for kindly bringing this point to light," the black horse said, relishing the moment. Then he turned his head and paced the floor to the far wall, where he stopped and commanded, "Map on!" In mid-air, blue fluorescent lines outlining a timeline appeared. As my eyes scanned the diagram in front of me, I recognized a few things.

The black horse turned and started presenting his evidence.

"The average person gets about 70 years or so here on what we affectionately call 'planet earth'. If you put that into sections," he paused, "you are approximately about mid-life right now," he continued, pointing to the timeline on the map with a long stick in his mouth.

"Wow. I've never looked at it that way or seen it so clearly before," I whispered to myself.

"So, according to averages and statistics, you have a good 45 years or so left. If we bring into consideration your excellent health and fitness, you could live to be 120. Or, if something drastic happens, you might not finish the year." The black horse chuckled to himself, making me feel very uncomfortable. His weather forecast-type point that 'anything can happen' lacked clarity.

"Where is this debate going?" Peacemaker interrupted.

"Can we get to the point?" the judge asked the black horse.

Without skipping a beat, the black horse cleared his throat, and then looked directly at me. "In this half life that you have lived, have you so far ever been without food, clothing, shelter, and water?"

"No."

"Have you ever been without anything that you needed?"

"No, I have always had everything that I needed and more. I mean, I dream of big crazy things, but they are certainly not needed or required..."

The black horse cut me off. Pointing the stick over the suspended timeline, he reiterated, "So, if we look back through your life, you have always gotten everything that you needed?"

"Yes."

In a booming voice, he emphasized his words. "And a lot of things that you wanted."

"Yes."

"So where does this scarcity limitation come from?"

Seeing where the black horse was going with his questions, I scrambled for words. "Well, ah, er." My head was spinning with this new way of looking at my beliefs around money. I grappled for an answer. "In case I ever don't have enough?"

Aware that I was caught off guard, the black horse swiftly moved to add yet another angle. Looking back at the map, which had turned into a video screen, I saw lots of smiling faces of children from Africa, their white teeth glowing.

"Do these children have more than you?"

"No."

The scene changed, showing how those people lived in their huts with little food and provisions, no running water, no shoes, and only a few articles of clothing, which they were wearing. I felt sick to my stomach at the thought that I could even feel any scarcity when I have so much compared to others. Seeing the reality of how others live in the images flashing in front of me, gave me another perspective. The clip ended and the black horse paused to let it sink in.

I felt bad, and could not think of anything to say, my head buzzing with thoughts. I had seen pictures before of how other people in the world live, but I had never been in a moment of scarcity when I was seeing them. Then I thought about how crazy that was.

Sensing that he had hit a home run on his point, the black horse called out, "Case one evidence is complete."

Guilty As Charged

There was a rumbling sound as the jury discussed the evidence that had just been laid out before them. The judge banged his mallet on the desk again, calling everyone to order and moving their attention to the next order of business.

"Let's move to case two. Un-thankfulness," the black horse continued. "Have you or have you not read the story in the Bible about how God took his people out of slavery and pointed them toward the Promised Land?"

"Yes," I replied.

"Did you or did you not read about the miracles that God performed for his people to do this?"

"Yes."

"Do you remember the piece where he enabled them to walk out of Egypt away from slavery and parted the Red Sea when their slave masters changed their minds and came after them? They walked away from danger. They were looked after and provided for. He gave them food from heaven, water from a rock. He took care of their every need. But they started to grumble and complain." The black horse stomped his feet to make his main point. "Did you or did you not read this story and feel appalled with how ungrateful they were? That they couldn't see what God was doing for them? They couldn't see the provision they had been given?"

"Yes, I did," I blurted out, feeling incredibly exposed.

"So you could see clearly, as a spectator or part of the jury in their lives, how unthankful they were?"

"I could," I reluctantly nodded in agreement. The black horse continued with a change of tack in his line of debate.

"A similar thing happened for you last Christmas, didn't it? While you were watching *The Christmas Story,*

the story of Ebenezer Scrooge? Watching that mean guy and what he was doing with his life, you said to yourself, 'How come he is so mean and uncaring?' Then as the ghosts took him through his life, he saw that he had no great reason to be so mean. He had no great reason to be so bitter. You found it difficult to identify with the guy. He was soooo mean and rude and unreasonable." The black horse paused and swallowed. "He has a massive life turnaround and goes the other way, sharing and giving and being. It is easy to be a good person living in the middle of Mr. Scrooge's two extremes, not a horrible or mean person, not a massively giving-my-life-to-a-cause person either. Just in the middle of the road."

The black horse's point felt like a knife piercing my heart. I felt completely exposed.

"When Mr. Scrooge started to see things differently and opened up, you were impressed with the big changes that he made, and thankful for the nice story with a good ending." The black horse paused for effect, and then drove the point home. "Can you or can you not see the correlation these stories have with yourself?" Not waiting for my answer, he continued. "It is easier to point the finger and see that others need to change, but it is not as easy to see the other four fingers pointing back at you when you are in your own stuff. You are comfortable and you live with it. It is so easy to sit in the stands and be an observer of other lives and talk about what they should or shouldn't do and how they should behave. *You* are Ebenezer Scrooge. *You* are just the same... Unthankful for all the things you have!"

I felt shocked and overwhelmed, but knew there was a strong part of what the black horse was saying that was absolutely true. I had no words to explain my case. I felt helpless and unworthy of anything. I hung my head in agreement with my offense.

"Yes, I can see that I am exactly the same."

"Case two evidence complete," the black horse stated with conviction.

The murmuring of the observers was muted. After a long pause, the black horse, enjoying how well and easy his points had been to make, turned to the judge.

"Continue to case three... Getting Comfortable," the judge instructed.

The black horse turned again to look at me as he continued. "Have you or have you not enjoyed settling down in the last two years?"

"Yes, I have," I replied in almost a whisper, not knowing what to expect next.

"Have you received a lot of creature comforts and things in your possession?"

"Yes, we have."

"So you could say you have gotten really comfortable?" The black horse asked as he wiggled his head in delight.

"Yes."

"So comfortable that you are slipping into a place of not wanting to move and break out again into new things?"

"Yes," I nodded again with my head hung low.

"Case three evidence complete."

The black horse walked over to the side of his table and took a sip of water out of the open water trough at its edge.

"Please continue to case four, Being Tight and Un-Giving" the judge said, looking at me as if I were already pronounced guilty. He seemed to want to speed up the

process and get to the sentencing portion of the proceeding.

The black horse changed tack again and continued in a singsong voice. "Giving to people money or time or good deeds or...? The debate is, how to give, when to give, whom to give to, why to give? This always brings up a lot of questions in your mind. Is it better to do something than just giving money? Writing a check can seem so heartless and removed, as opposed to actually going and doing something for someone. The questions can get you all caught up in the whys and wherefores and stop you from actually doing anything. Would it be fair to say that you have gotten so caught up in what is the right thing to do that you often don't do anything at all?"

Feeling exceptionally awful, with my head hung even lower, I replied, "Yes."

"Case four evidence complete," the black horse stated simply.

The air in the courtroom could have been cut with a knife. Interrupting the silence, the judge stated, "Case five... Unappreciative and Not Celebrating."

"Did you or did you not try to shirk off your birthdays and not tell anyone about them?"

"Yes."

"Have you or have you not been unappreciative of what you have in your life?"

I sat back to think. "Have I?"

"Have you taken the time to celebrate the great things that are happening in your life on a daily basis?"

"Not always," I acknowledged.

"Have you always openly accepted gifts and appreciated them in your life?"

"No, not always," I acquiesced.

"Case five evidence complete," the black horse said as he lifted his head high in the air. Addressing the jury with a pleased and arrogant tone, he declared, "Now that all the evidence has been laid out, I would propose that Rachel is guilty of five charges: Scarcity, Unthankfulness, Getting Comfortable, Being Tight and Un-Giving, and Unappreciative and Not Celebrating."

"Please stand and declare whether you are guilty or not guilty of these five charges as set out before you today," the judge said in his booming voice.

I slowly stood, my knees shaking and my head hung in shame. I knew the answer that I had to give. Picking up my energy and courage, I took a deep breath and opened my mouth to respond.

Before I could continue, Peacemaker's voice declared, "Wait!" I saw that my necklace had started to glow bright red, lighting up the entire courtroom. Peacemaker continued, "It would seem that there is more evidence to come."

Seeing Things Through Heaven's Eyes

"Let the necklace speak," the judge announced.

"Evidence for Getting Comfortable," Peacemaker added as the scene unfolded like a hologram in front of everyone in the courtroom.

Tears were forming in my eyes, as I was moved to emotion. "You cannot walk on water if you do not get out of the boat," Don said with his big deep blue eyes glazing with emotion. His analogy resonated with me, since walking on water represents so many scary things in my life. Don and I have an incredible life with so much, and we had gotten to a nice comfort level. "It is time to get out of the boat," he continued.

"Go hard or go home," I said, nodding my head.

"Go hard or go home," he repeated in agreement. "It is time to get out of the boat. No holding back. No living with limits. Let's do it. Let's go for it."

"Alright," I agreed. We hugged. I felt supported and so warm and comfortable in Don's arms as our excitement about our decision to move forward and go and do what we have not gone and done before grew.

The necklace flashed. I felt great and thankful that the necklace reminded me of where we were heading.

Peacemaker looked alive and engaged in the process, like he was unable to help me previously, but had hit his stride.

The necklace flashed again and Peacemaker called out, "Evidence for Being Tight and Un-Giving."

Don was reading the verse in Matthew 25: 35-40: "'For I was hungry and you gave me something to eat, I was thirsty and you gave me something to drink, I was a stranger and you invited me in, I needed clothes and you clothed me, I was sick and you looked after me, I was in prison and you came to visit me.

" 'Then the righteous will answer him, 'Lord, when did we see you hungry and feed you, or thirsty and give you something to drink? When did we see you a stranger and invite you in, or needing clothes and clothe you? When did we see you sick or in prison and go to visit you?'

" 'The King will reply, 'I tell you the truth, whatever you did for one of the least of these brothers of mine, you did for me.' "

Don looked up and said, "This is what it is all about. Let's plan on some way to help and share and start to be that in our lives."

Unsure of what this was going to look like, but realizing that we had shifted a huge paradigm in our lives, we were excited for the change.

"This is what life is all about, giving and sharing with others, helping others along the road. Life has so much more meaning when you are giving and sharing."

Don nodded in agreement, and then suggested, "Let's start a new family tradition and give to something or someone who is doing some of these things."

"Yes, let's do that. What about Ingela and Richard and their 'Horses for Orphans' project? I love what they are doing."

"Yeah, that's a great idea," Don replied.

"Their passion and dedication is awesome. They are giving their time and resources to orphan kids. They have done amazing things in Africa and are now moving into Brazil and India. Ingela and Richard are great friends of ours who just exemplify God's love and giving. I am blown away by their ability to do amazing things in their lives. They show what it means to get out of the boat and walk on water. They gave their lives to God and work for free. They receive donations that seem to cover most things they need. The rest is covered by some of their savings.

"They have gifted horses to orphan children who have never seen horses before. What they are doing gives the orphans purpose, teaches life skills, and shows how to take care of something precious. Now that is dedication at a whole new level."

Tears started to fill my eyes as I thought about giving, and even more, of making a trip to one of their projects to help out, to take Shona so she could experience helping out at a whole other level. "We just have to do this," I insisted to Don.

We went straight to the computer and donated online.

The necklace flashed again.

Peacemaker asked me directly, "So what did you do after donating online?"

"We were so incredibly inspired, we wanted to do more."

"What did you do?"

I smiled, brightening at the thought. "We wrote up in our business plan that 10 percent of our profits are to go to this cause," I explained.

Peacemaker turned to the judge and said, "Evidence of Giving complete."

The jury murmured, but this time the change in the atmosphere was positive.

"Case three, Unappreciative and Not Celebrating," Peacemaker called out while looking directly at the necklace. It opened up the next story.

"What are your five successes today?" Don asked me. I thought for a few moments, and easily came up with five things that I felt were successful that day. Feeling positive, we headed off to sleep. As I waited to drop off into slumber land, I went through my day in my head like I always do. In my head, my thoughts continued. *I should have said... to such and such, and oh, I forgot to get this thing for this person, and...*

So not only was I tired from the day, I had completely derided myself for what I could have done better.

My necklace flashed, zipping us out of that scene directly into another.

A few days later, Don asked, "What are your five successes today?"

"I don't want to do that today," I snapped. "I haven't had a good day."

"I know," Don said, patiently, "but we committed to doing this 90 day challenge, and today is the day that you need to do this the most."

Now I was annoyed that I had not only had a bad day, but I had to think of five successes as well. "I don't have any," I said, while my brain and emotions resisted changing the state I was in.

"There must be something that was successful?" Don prodded.

I stomped into the bedroom, completely not in the mood. But realizing that Don was serious about this, I yelled back to him, "I got up!"

"Yes," Don replied. "What else?" he encouraged me.

"I showered." Seeing the humor in what I was coming up with, I felt myself lightening up.

"Good," he replied.

"I went to work," I continued. "I think that you should thank me for giving you three today, as I didn't think there were any."

"Okay," Don conceded, knowing not to push it too far.

The scene faded out.

Peacemaker cleared his throat and asked me, "Can you remember what happened after you finished that 90 day challenge?"

"Yes, I do. I cannot remember exactly when it happened, but there was a transition as our focus shifted to more positive things. I was able to come up with successes so much more easily. In fact, they were a bigger focus for me."

"What about your beating yourself up each night?"

"That is quite amazing. I'm not sure exactly when it happened after the challenge, but I did not beat myself up each night anymore about what I should have or could have done in a day. It helped me to see the positives that happened each day and to concentrate my attention on them. Funny enough, I seem to have more positive days now that I focus on better things."

"Now tell us about your last birthday," Peacemaker continued.

A smile lit up across my face. "It was wonderful. I celebrated it, telling people about it, and I received many gifts. If felt good. I had a wonderful time."

"Excellent," Peacemaker replied, nodding his head. "What else?"

"We bought new wine glasses."

The jury murmured. The black horse yelled, "I object! Relevance? They don't even drink wine!"

"Make a point or move on," the judge bellowed.

Peacemaker nodded to me.

"You are right, we don't actually drink wine. Instead, we put water in the glasses because we call them our celebration glasses and use them to toast to the awesome things that have happened in a week, or when there is a special occasion."

"Thank you." Peacemaker lowered his head with subdued delight. "There is more…"

"More," I repeated out loud, then a big smile came to my face as the necklace enveloped us in a new scene.

With a final push that released the pain, Shona Angelina Jessop entered the world. I took in a great breath of relief.

"It's a girl!" Don declared. I smiled, delighted, as I had always wanted a little girl. There were smiles all around as Don placed our little girl on my chest. She was perfect, so small she took my breath away. Time stood still. I just stared at her for hours, soaking her up.

We floated out of the scene. I was overwhelmed, with tears in my eyes as I relived that special time. "What an amazing joy, an amazing creation. It doesn't get any better than that. I celebrated that special day with my fantastic husband who was by my side the entire way. My best friend, Shona, had flown all the way from New

Zealand to share this incredible moment with us. Our daughter's birth was a most amazing celebration and a wonderful gift that we have in our lives.

"Speaking of gifts, it was also amazing to tell my friend that we were going to name our daughter Shona. She was incredibly delighted. Everything was perfect," I said with tears rolling down my cheeks. I was happy to let everyone see the joy that I still felt from that moment.

Peacemaker was enjoying the scene as much as I was. "Evidence for Celebration is complete. Now to Un-thankfulness." Peacemaker motioned to the necklace, which flashed its light across the room, embracing us in the next scene.

Standing on my own with my arms stretched out wide in our house, I slowly turned around, looking at the room. "I am so thankful for my life. Thank you for my family, the things we have and the love we share, the people we know and the lessons we have learned." I turned some more, seeing and thinking of all the wonderful things that we have, and feeling incredibly blessed. "I am so thankful for the learning and the blessings, and... Thank you." Taking in some deep, soft, relaxed, and thankful breaths, I continued. "I receive all these blessings. I love all the wonderful gifts that you have given us. Thank you."

My necklace flashed away from the scene.

Peacemaker, enjoying seeing the tables turn, walked back to his spot as the jury whispered in hushed tones. After what seemed like an eternity, a squirrel darted and zipped all the way to the judge and whispered in his ear. The judge stood up and in a big voice, said, "We have come to some final conclusions. On the stand today is Rachel, who is being tried for five different charges:

Scarcity, Un-thankfulness, Getting Comfortable, Tight and Un-Giving, and Unappreciative and Not Celebrating. It has been unanimously decided. On four charges of Un-thankfulness, Getting Comfortable, Being Tight and Un-Giving, and Unappreciative and Not Celebrating, we have cleared your name and declared you, 'Not guilty'."

I took a big sigh and relaxed in my chair.

"However, the charge of Scarcity is still open for debate," the judge continued.

I had felt incredibly relieved to have seen the clips from the necklace, and to have my name cleared of four charges. But I felt the tension start to build up, knowing that scarcity was something that had come up for me again and again.

Then the black horse stood. He began to question me again, knowing that this was his last chance to declare me guilty. "Did you or did you not sell everything and risk it all to come over to the States?" he said, pointing his nose at the timeline.

"Yes, I did," I replied, feeling good about my having broken out of that comfort zone.

"Was it, or was it not the best thing you ever did in your life to that point?"

"Yes, it was."

"Would you have the life that you have now if you hadn't done that?"

"No, I would not."

"Can you see that risking it all was actually a blessing?"

"Yes," I replied, surprised that he was asking encouraging questions. Then he hit me right where it hurt.

"Why did you decide to hold onto your scarcity again and again, and not allow yourself to have this and more in the future?"

I felt the atmosphere in the room rise, especially under my warm, brown cloak.

Not giving me time to answer, the black horse fired the next question at me. "Are you letting scarcity rule your life?"

"Yes," I blurted out, feeling the shame of the pattern that had been a strong part of my life.

"Guilty as charged!" he yelled while walking back to his desk, slamming his large book shut with his nose, then motioning with his head toward the map, which disappeared.

"Wait!" I shouted. "What if I am ready to live where nothing holds me back, and let go of scarcity?"

The black horse looked up. The jury stopped and looked at me, then to the judge, and finally to Peacemaker. Stunned at my own outbreak, but ready to put it all on the line, I stood up and declared, "I am ready to look at my life through heaven's eyes. To take another leap of faith. Do you remember that I went through that waterfall for this necklace? I jumped with Peacemaker off a huge ledge, not knowing what would happen to us. I used the hairbrush and was able to tap into my inner beauty. I pushed through my own invisible walls. I started to ask the right questions. I risked it all to come to the States and, thankfully, met the love of my life. My life is not scarce. I am blessed and loved. I live in abundance."

Pointing to where the map had been, it appeared again. "I do not have much time left on this earth, considering the 70 year or so average," I continued. "It is time to risk it all and go to the next level."

Peacemaker nodded his head while watching me speak. The black horse let out a distressed grunt.

"I am ready to celebrate more. I am ready to receive all the blessings and love that is coming my way. I am thankful for my life."

The jury all stood and clapped and stomped loudly, with what looked to me like huge smiles on their faces as they started to yell and holler in their own unique voices. The judge, un-moved, motioned to the jury to settle down.

"This is all good and great for you to say in this moment, but how are you going to keep this emotional high? How are you going to live this in your life?"

I paused to think. The jury all leaned toward me, waiting to hear my reply.

My necklace interrupted the moment, trying to show me something. We all saw a picture where I was caught in my pattern of scarcity. But there was something different about it.

"I am tired of this feeling, and this place that I go of feeling like I don't have enough," the image of me in the scene said. "I remember a book that I was reading just the other day. Its theme was, 'stop speaking the lies'. I realize now that I've been thinking and speaking out the lies of scarcity!" my double said aloud. "I am blocking my ability to receive. I am the one keeping us in this place!"

My head continued to fire this new information at my body double, but I was no longer able to say anything out loud. Arrrrgh! I was caught between two worlds, my habituated pattern, and the new paradigm I wanted so much to embrace. Everything seemed to slow down as I

imagined there were two people, one sitting on each of my shoulders, like the cartoons of an angel and a devil.

The devil character, with a smooth, charming voice, said, "But we don't have enough!"

The angel character, with a sweet and soothing voice, said, "Have you ever been without anything that you need?"

The bantering went back and forth for some time until I said, "Enough! I am going to believe the truth that we are going to be okay!" I firmly stated, speaking to the small people on my shoulders.

I shook my head, and said, "I don't believe this just happened."

In that moment, a feeling of peace consumed me and I felt ready to let go of scarcity, with a clear and deep knowing that I will always be okay, that I am well looked after.

The necklace launched us into a new scene. Sitting still and breathing, obviously in a better state, I was telling Don what had happened. "When you told me about needing to buy something, it totally sent me into scarcity. While I was in that state, I started to hear my inner dialogue spout lots of negative things, saying things like, 'Oh my gosh, that is too expensive. We can't afford it. What about our expenses?' and on and on.

"I realized that what I was doing was not only feeling scarce, I was affirming scarcity in my inner thoughts. There is no way that we can move on or be free of this place while I am holding us back with these limiting thoughts. I have to change my language. I have to stop speaking these lies and start to say and believe that we can have anything we want. Instead of immediately moving into scarcity, I want to say, 'Let's check our budget and see how we can fit it in and make it work. It just might not happen today.'"

"That is awesome. I love that. What a great realization," Don replied. "Only speak where you want to be, not where you are."

As we came out of the story and the necklace returned to its beautiful silvery white color, Peacemaker seemed pleased with the last images.

But the black horse probed deeper. "How are you going to make this a reality and seal it in your life?"

Before I was able to answer, my necklace again helped explain my story.

My head was spinning again, telling me lies about how things are and what I should and shouldn't do. I took in some deep breaths and started to pray, staying open and in my heart. What a magical morning. I was running through the woods, seeing birds flying through the air, and then I ran past some squirrels playing in the trees. Turning a corner through the woods, I spooked a few deer. They ran off ahead of me. Feeling like I was in a movie with all this wild life, a smile came to my face.

I stated my affirmations. "I am living where nothing is holding me back," I said with vigor. "There is no reason I can't do it," I said, my energy lifting as my state of mind changed with the truth and reality of who I am. "I attract loving, supportive, and emotionally fit people into my life. I am beautiful. Our worth is beyond imagination. I am claiming the moment. The timing in our lives is always perfect. We expect and get only the best. The right horses are coming into our lives."

As I told myself these words, I felt certainty, with more clarity flowing through me. My cloudy head had become clear and focused, ready for a new day.

In fact, I felt brilliant as I jumped over a few logs on the ground, running around several trees. I reached the river's edge and stopped, opening my arms out to my sides. I breathed in and received the beauty and love that was flowing and ready for me. I yelled in my head, *I am ready to receive all the love and blessings that you have for me!* I touched my heart and repeated, *I am ready to receive all the love and blessings that you have for me!*

Being in nature had restored and uplifted me, moving my body and putting me in a peak state. I felt wonderful. *It is so good to be alive and moving.*

As I came out of the picture, I could see that the black horse was not fully convinced by the images he had just witnessed. He continued his line of questioning. "So are your affirmations working for you?"

"Yes, they are. I have certainly learned a lot about them. I have had to experiment with them."

"Experiment?"

"Yes. Let me give you an example. I used to say 'I am beautiful'. I said that because I did not believe it. I repeated this statement for about six months. Some changes did happen slowly over that time. I could say it and believe it when I was in a very peak state. I could start to say things like, 'I have beautiful hair; I am unique and precious.' So, things were changing, but I still had backchat on that main affirmation itself."

"Backchat?"

"Yes. I would say I am beautiful, and my backchat, my inner dialogue, would be like that little angel or devil sitting on my shoulder commenting on the things that I was saying, like 'Oh yeah? Not compared to others' or 'In what way?' Then the angel would cut in. 'Beauty is in the eye of the beholder.' Often, the devil would win and I would affirm that belief. Listening to all of my backchat, I undid a lot of the good of saying and hearing the positive affirmation, which I couldn't quite believe and agree with.

"Don found some keys for me. First, to find an affirmation that you can agree with and affirm, that has no backchat possibility. That way, when you say the affirmation, it is empowering and the little guy doesn't have anything much to say about it. With no backchat to get in the way, you embrace the belief and it gives you energy, peace, and/or resourcefulness. It makes a huge difference in your life to get a dose of the truth."

"What is an example of a no-backchat affirmation?"

"Well it will be different for everybody, because we have different beliefs, but the affirmation that I found along the same lines on beauty is, 'I am emanating beauty from the inside out.'"

"How is that helpful?"

"Well, when I say that, I have no backchat. I agree with the statement and it makes me feel good about myself. So it feels empowering."

"But does it make any difference?"

I smiled. "The next trick is to install the affirmation in yourself. I needed to hear and affirm that affirmation more than I heard and fed myself with negative affirmations. Most females would agree, every time you look at a few magazines, you can go into an 'I am not beautiful' place. If you have an affirmation to help you in those extreme circumstances and you install it in your mind, it then starts to become your reality."

"How can affirmations become your reality?"

"By saying them out loud and listening to them on an audio device every day. Over time it really sinks in and it

is who you are and what you believe. It has really helped me to swing the pendulum, hearing and listening to more positive things in my life than the negative. It helps me to make changes in my life.

"I am ready to proclaim what I am, who I am. The real me. The me who is free of restrictions and limitation!" I declared.

The jury stood again, and this time clapped as Peacemaker nodded in agreement with my proclamation.

The judge loudly said, "Not guilty!"

The jury stomped and clapped even louder, with a few shouts and whistles as I stood up.

The black horse looked at me. "This is not the end of this," he threatened, then turned and galloped out of the courtroom, the back doors automatically swinging open for him, then closing again after he left. His words struck fear into my core. I felt a rock in the pit of my stomach. Then I shrugged it off and turned around, stepped down from the witness stand, and ran to Peacemaker. I closed my eyes as I gave him a big warm hug, remembering who I am and who I was becoming.

"Thank you. I needed to see that from a different perspective."

"You are most welcome," Peacemaker said, his warm familiar voice giving me a feeling of comfort. As I opened my eyes and looked back around the room, the judge and jury and my cloak had disappeared. We were back in the woods again, just as before.

"Wow, that was intense," Peacemaker affirmed in a slow, strong voice. "Don't ever forget who you are."

I nodded as I gulped, pressing my lips together, with emotion welling up inside me.

"Thanks."

Dream Warrior

"Let's walk. We still have some places to be," Peacemaker advised. I felt incredibly powerful and genuine, knowing I had conquered some huge things in my life. As we walked along through some more woods, I heard the sound of rushing water. In a short time, we came to a great river.

The rushing water was clear. Peacemaker and I looked at the surroundings. There is something restoring about moving water. In fact, water of any kind is like that. We walked closer, and then out on the big rocks on the edge of the rushing water.

We both drank deeply of the fresh water. There is nothing quite like that feeling.

"Oh, that feels much better," I said as I sat down on the rocks to enjoy watching the water moving around and cascading over the rocks on its way downstream.

Peacemaker walked a short distance into the water and stood there. I had a feeling of suspicion that he was up to no good. For good reason, as the next moment he pawed his foot into the water, splashing me.

"Oh!" I exclaimed as the cool water splashed on me. I jumped up and moved over to the side to splash him

back. We were soon engaged in a good old water fight. After becoming drenched and having a good laugh, Peacemaker stopped.

"We need to cross this river, and seeing that we are already wet, let's go!"

"Okay," I agreed, jumping up on Peacemaker who carried me across the river. The current was strong and we angled just slightly upstream to ensure hitting the flow at the correct angle. When we got to the other side, I slipped off his back and sat on the river rocks, drying off in the sun.

"Thanks, I needed that."

"It's good to have some fun after that really intense court hearing."

"Yes sirree, it sure is."

"But there is more, isn't there?" Peacemaker suggested.

"When you start a healing process, sometimes you do not realize how much more there is. In fact, it never stops. But the good news is every little bit just makes life so much better. I am thankful for my horse, who helps me to live the dream."

"Tell me about Dreamy," Peacemaker asked as he stood in front of me and lowered his head to my eye level.

"Dreamy is the most special horse I have ever had. He is a bright light, a shining star. He has helped me to live many of my dreams. Playing with him at liberty is so incredibly fun.

"Putting it all together, the years of training me, then training him to get that connection where there is an understanding of each other's body language, then adding new cues that we have formed together, has been an incredible journey," I explained.

As I talked, my necklace lit up and I saw a reflection of Dreamy and me in Peacemaker's eye as we were dashed to a new scene.

I was asking Dreamy for a maneuver and he responded with willingness and a huge effort. It was a dance where we come together and connect and flow, bridging the gap between horse and human communication. Feeling the exuberance and his effort to try touched my heart and made me feel alive, relishing the dream and the love and the moment together.

My emotions were running high as I enjoyed the feeling of connection with his spirit. I balanced asking for things, then giving him reward and release. The beauty of it as it began to come together was awe-inspiring.

Catching and holding his attention and energy, we flowed together with an idea. I moved my energy up and down to accentuate the communication of when we moved and when we stopped. That connection was like an unseen band of light between us. When it was strong it was like there was nothing else. We concentrated on each other feeling our every move. The intensity of our dance was strong. Even when we moved together in unison, the dance was always different.

My senses came alive hearing his breathing and footfalls. I saw Dreamy, not only physically, but also in my mind's eye when he was behind me. I could feel what Dreamy was doing and also how he was feeling, if he was braced and tight or having fun and being exuberant.

After enjoying being with him on the ground, I jumped on him, loving feeling him under me. As I balanced on his back with nothing to hold me on, I felt every muscle and movement beneath me, like his legs became my legs. Moving with my energy and weight, he

responded with a flying lead change, then into a beautiful elevated trot. We cantered around together, enjoying the moment. I concentrated on keeping our energy and presence full and real, loving the relationship and joy that we gave to each other.

As I played and moved with Dreamy I realized that it doesn't matter what I do now or in the future with horses. I had made it. Having excelled with my Natural Horsemanship goals, I was living my dream. I was thankful to my horses and my teachers for helping me get there.

Sprinkling shards of light brought us back to the present.

"What a blessing. If that wasn't enough, I can ride him bareback and bridle-less, walking, trotting, and cantering around, going up and down hills, over banks and jumping fences. We do flying lead changes and I can get him to stop by just bringing my life down, breathing out. That is so awesome. Stunning and amazing, really. I can do all the things I saw on the inspiring video all those years ago. And more!

"Horses have taught me how to be in the moment, how to think less and be more. Dreamy has called me to a higher place. His spirit calls me to do more, to dance together, something that I constantly have to feel completely free to do naturally. To let go and flow, and let the spirit move me. To allow the wonder and beauty to flow in my life. That is what I was aiming for."

"Time to add a new addition to the family," Peacemaker said, interrupting me.

"Huh?" I replied, caught off guard with his statement, as the necklace's love embraced us again. We dropped into a new scene.

To Be An Olympian

There she was, a picture of beauty. Watching her move took my breath away. She almost floated through the air, with her beautiful, big fluid strides. Mesmerized, I felt like I could watch her move all day. As if her movement was not enough to completely captivate me, her personality bubbled as she tossed her head and played back with me.

Sand flicked through the air, her hair flying as she glided across the arena. The sun was shining on 16 hands of beautiful bay with black mane, tail, legs, and ears. She glistened in the light.

Light on her feet, she seemed to hang in the air for a very long time, with great rhythm. I felt like at any moment she would do something different, just for fun.

Her curiosity took over and she turned toward me to see what I might do next, and if we would play some more or if she could change the game up. I put energy toward her and she jumped her front end away from it as though it were a tangible thing. Then she shot off down to the other side of the arena to stop and look back, waiting for more.

We flashed out of the arena, and back to the path.

"Diamond Lilly. I have watched her granddad for years, and had written on my Dream Horse list that I wanted a horse like him. What an opportunity to find this beautiful horse that has natural talent in the areas I am interested, no limitations on look or movement or quality or... or anything."

Before I knew it we were flashed into another scene.

The anticipation as we were taking the big drive to Silverhorne Sporthorses in Sacramento to pick up Diamond caused my head to spin about the decision to get a new horse. I wasn't sure if I was worthy of such a fantastic horse. All that she had, would I do her justice? Would I be good enough to take her all the way to the top of competition, where I wanted to go?

There would be nothing holding me back with this horse. There would be no excuses of bad previous training or having to teach her how to canter. She was brilliant. Spending time, starting her, putting on a foundation, and then going for it was all I needed to do.

I really had to battle with my head about being worthy of this horse, of having time to work with Diamond the way she would need to be worked. In addition, the financial obligation pushed all my scarcity buttons again. After much time and debate, I knew it was the right timing, and my affirmation to be ready to accept all the wonder and beauty that God has for us enabled me to accept this gift with open arms.

The necklace brought me back again.

"Well, you did it!" Peacemaker observed.

Yes, I openly received this beautiful gift. I love having Diamond at home, to just watch her in the field."

"It's changed some things in you though, hasn't it?"

I reflected for a moment. "Yes, it really has. Now I have the horse. I have to personally take the next step up."

"What is the next step for you?"

"I have wanted to compete at the Olympics since I was 13 years old. I watched the top horse riders compete in the Games and was captivated by what they could do, how cool they were. I remember watching Mark Todd win Gold for New Zealand in the Eventing. I had tears in my eyes I was so proud. That little horse Charisma jumped his heart out. What a hero. It was an awesome thing to watch. It instilled in me how I wanted to do the same."

"So Mark Todd was your hero?"

"Yes, I guess he was. But as I grew older I realized that Olympic Eventing was a grueling sport at the top levels and I was not so sure that was what I wanted my horse to do, after watching a few horrific deaths of both people and horses. A mistake can be fatal when going at such great speeds and over such large fences."

"You didn't want that dream anymore?"

"I still wanted to compete, but just not in Eventing. Stadium jumping briefly crossed my mind, but Dressage has always been really intriguing. It used to be my weakest phase when Eventing, so I put a lot more time into it and started to love it more and more as I learned and grew in this area. I also couldn't even fathom how people were doing some of the moves they were getting their horses to do.

"Time has passed and I have taught and ridden all of the moves I had once only been able to admire. I feel like I have achieved many dreams. In fact, now that I am living my dream of connection and bond I feel ready to go after my next dream. I feel like my foundation is really solid."

"But, you have the horse. Is there still something missing?"

"I can't say that I'm an Olympian, even though I've accomplished much of my other dreams. But how do you become one if you are not one?"

My necklace dropped us into another scene.

Don and I were in a deep discussion.

"So what do you want to achieve?" Don asked me.

"I want to be an Olympian."

"Why?"

"I want to prove…" I stopped in mid-sentence.

"Prove what?"

I shrugged. "I don't know. The reasons I initially had for wanting this were that I wanted to prove I was excellent, good, and okay. Now those things are not relevant for me. I feel really good about myself. And having healed my heart in so many areas, I just do not need to prove anything anymore." I paused. "Wow, that is a huge realization."

"So why do you want to be an Olympian now?"

"I'll have to think about that," I said, searching my mind for an answer. "I know," I continued. "Because I said I was going to, so I want to finish that and prove my dream to myself."

Don smiled at me, loving the way I find answers to a question I thought I had all sewn up, but now had no bearing on where I was in my life.

"Because I want to wave the Natural Horsemanship flag, showing that you can do beautiful things with a horse without force, fear, and intimidation," I continued.

To Be An Olympian

"And to ride for God, using music and beauty to show his love to others."

"Those are better reasons," Don replied. "This dream, this goal started from a place of all about you, and turned into a goal for others."

Feeling light and encouraged, I replied, "It did, didn't it?"

"So what is holding you back from achieving this?"

"Well nothing. I have a really good plan and I'm on my way. I see that it is going to happen. I just cannot call myself an Olympian because I have not been to an Olympics."

"I beg to differ. You are an Olympian. You have just not competed at an Olympics yet. You are showing Natural Horsemanship and how you can help people to be better with their horses. You are on your way. You are awesome. You do not need to do this to get love anymore. The difference is that now you are doing this to give. You are free from boundaries and free to push forward. *You are an Olympian*," Don emphasized.

As I heard those words ringing in my ears, for the first time I felt like I could grab a hold of that and receive it and *be* that, and let my light shine.

"Stop tying love to significance. Become the Olympian inside," Don continued.

"That makes sense. I am getting to a place where nothing is required of me. Isn't that enlightenment, where you come to a place of being?" I wondered out loud.

As Don continued, my heart and soul received his encouraging words. "You don't have to be anything to be loved. You are already loved. You are an Olympian. You are a lover. You are a wife. You are a mother. You are not

all that other stuff. You may feel things like being tired and exhausted, but you are loved. You do not need the world to tell you that. Everything will turn out exactly how it is supposed to be, a life without that fear, without a need to have the world tell you who you are."

"I need to tell the world who I am. Outside influences do not define me, I do. I am passionate. I am energetic. I do not agree with the lies rolling around in my head. I am unstoppable."

"Yes, you are," Don agreed.

"Now, I just have to hold onto this, to go have fun and enjoy the ride on the way to my dreams."

The scene dissolved.

My Mentor

"What an encouragement from Don and a change in my thinking that was. I felt like my heart was stronger and more whole."

"You have healed so much," Peacemaker observed.

"Yes, it is a massive growing experience and fortunately, I have had some really good mentors to help me along the way."

"Sometimes the mentorship that we want in life comes to us in very different ways," Peacemaker said. "Who is your biggest mentor right now?"

"That is easy. Our daughter, Shona Angelina."

The necklace popped us into the next scene.

Melting my heart, there she went into that life-freezing giggle. Her laugh gets me every time. I was taken by the moment and I breathed deeply, enjoying and taking pleasure in that special time by giving her a little tickle and joining in the fun. She was running around like a zealous person, like how a person should be when they are free of all inhibitions, living in their heart and truly being present in the moment. Like a child.

How can you be in a hurry and in your head, moving too fast and trying to get things done that you think are important at the time, when reminded of the purity that

she displays? When that laugh starts, dabbed with little shrieks of delight, it reminds me of what is truly important. Shona's energy lights the world wherever she goes.

As I watched her in the scene, she found something incredibly amusing. Her huge smile captivated me and her enjoyment of every aspect of life left me in want of more of that for my life. *She lives in the moment,* I thought to myself. *Aren't I meant to be the parent teaching my child? She is certainly teaching me so much. I don't even know where to begin.*

I was drawn to so much about her. There she went again. There was nothing, absolutely nothing, holding her back. She was completely free. As I watched her finding absolute delight in the smallest things, I saw her living in that beautiful place where nothing is holding her back. I want that more for my life. I let myself go and enjoyed being in the moment, laughing at the joy.

We soared out of the scene.

"What a wonderful gift she is. I hope to help her stay in that place and join in it more often myself," I said.

"Continue to breathe in that beautiful gift that you have been given," Peacemaker said.

"Yes, I am very thankful for her. I sometimes find it hard to believe that I am actually a mum and that I am giving her so much, when I feel like it is actually the other way around. What a joy!"

Peacemaker and I lay down in the grass, which was dry from the sun's warm rays. I looked up into the blue sky and watched a few puffy clouds go slowly floating by, observing the pink, red, and orange colors starting to fill the edge of the sky. All the stories and experiences we'd had settled into my thoughts. The quiet was peaceful and fulfilling.

We watched the herd grazing in the distance, enjoying the warm late afternoon sun. It was perfect there. I let out a sigh and took in some big, satisfying breaths.

"Shona is just like the horses. Living free and un-abandoned," I commented.

"Yes, she is," Peacemaker agreed.

Facing My Fears

"My friend, the time has come. We must get you home. You need to take this necklace with you and get back to your woods before dark."

"I nearly forgot about that. But what happens if we don't get back before dark?"

"You will not remember this whole adventure or take the discoveries with you. Your heart will not be able to take this healing with you, and you will not have completed your quest. You will be as I met you this morning," he explained.

"You mean I will fail the quest because I will not know how to live with nothing holding me back?"

"You got it."

"I'll be sad to leave you Peacemaker, but I do want to get back to my family. And I do want to hold all of what I've learned today in my heart."

"You won't be leaving me. I am always with you," he replied. "Come on. Let's go."

I jumped up on Peacemaker. Every time I had done this, I'd received a little adrenaline buzz. Being on this big, powerful, and free animal was always a joy. I refocused as we headed off at a fast pace toward the woods that would take me home.

Facing My Fears

We covered the meadow quickly, then through some more woods, negotiating the trees and track with twists and turns. I could see another clearing coming up.

"I'm excited to get home and tell everyone about my adventures and all the things I have learned. Peacemaker, I am just so thankful for you," I said.

"Thanks. I appreciate you, too."

As soon as the words came out of his mouth the atmosphere changed dramatically, as we reached the next clearing. We heard the shrill cry of an anguished horse. Then out of the opposite woods and into the clearing galloped the black horse straight toward us. He stopped twenty feet away and snorted, the sound breaking through my confidence of getting home, as the whites of his eyes were blazing. He pawed the ground with intensity and looked directly into my eyes.

"Don't come this way," he said in a deep, strong voice. The intensity of his stare seemed to pierce my eyes, hurting my head. Yet I couldn't seem to tear my gaze away from him.

Peacemaker turned away from the other horse, alleviating the extreme gaze and giving me a break from the intense moment. He turned his head back toward me and said, "Rachel, all you have to do is get past that horse and to the edge of the woods before the last light of day fades, and you will have conquered your quest."

I glanced up to see the sun setting. "Get past that horse?" I said with doubt. "How am I going to do that?"

Peacemaker talked directly to me in a strong voice. "He is your fear. He is what drives you and what scares you. I cannot help you with this. I am unable to fight him for you. You have to face him alone. But know that I am with you in spirit."

I gulped, knowing that what Peacemaker had said was true. I slid down off of Peacemaker's back and he moved away.

Peacemaker slowly moved to the side, not wanting to leave me on my own for this part of my quest, but knowing that is what he must do if I was going to break through to another level in my life.

I turned to look at the line in the woods that I had to get to, and was quickly distracted by the flaring nostrils of the black horse. He was intimidating. I tried to breathe deeply, feeling incredibly inadequate to even be standing there at that moment.

"Turn around," he taunted. "You know you can't pass me. You're on your own. I'll make it easy on you. Turn around now, and you will have an easy time sliding back into your world the way you were before."

I felt compelled to listen and do exactly what he said. I thought to myself, *How am I going to get past this big strong horse with his massive intention?*

"I want to take these memories with me," I whispered as I plucked up all my courage and walked toward him. The atmosphere was so thick you could cut the air with a knife.

Then, he doubled the force by running hard toward me. The sound of his hooves on the hard ground made me feel faint. Fretting, I put my hands up to protect myself as I moved my head out of the way. At the last second, he stopped and breathed down into my face and neck. I'm sure he smelled my anxiety and the fear in my body. I slowly opened my eyes, seeing that he was only inches away from my face.

He startled me as he said, "I could kill you right now. *TURN AROUND!*" The words reverberated through my body and I cowered inside, terrified of this big black horse. I was frightened, but even with the fear, I knew that I was more afraid of not making it than I was of this obstacle.

I was in a Catch-22 situation, which paralyzed my ability to act at all. The black horse, seeing my indecision, reared up with his hooves flailing in the air, his muscles rippling. Self-preservation took over and I jumped to the side as fast and quick as I could, falling as I landed. I watched his hooves fall to the ground right where I was just a few moments before. I looked over at the spot I needed to get to, determined to make my quest.

I got up and ran forward. He galloped around in front of me and grabbed my dress with his teeth, lifting me off the ground.

"You will not make it home," he warned.

Terror ran through me again. I realized I only had one option to try to move forward. He tossed his head, throwing me into the air. I landed heavily on my bottom. As I felt the impact ricochet through my body, I blocked it out. I got up again and ran hard. He quickly scooted in front of me, blocking my way again, like a horse cutting a cow, ready to move to either side in an instant.

I gathered my courage. Knowing that a horse's reactions are much faster than a human's, I backed up as fast as I could, drawing him toward me. Then I stopped. The black horse slammed on his brakes, going into a slide stop. That was my chance. While he was sliding I had a few seconds to run past him. I was now only 10 feet from my goal and running. I glanced at the sun sinking beyond the horizon.

The black horse was not leaving anything to chance. He galloped up behind me as I was running and knocked

me to the ground with his head as he pulled up. I felt myself lose balance and fall forward, putting out my hands to lessen the impact of the fall. Then I felt the weight of his hoof firmly on my back.

"You are not going anywhere now," he said with a wicked delight in his voice. I felt defeated, resting my head on the ground. I didn't make it. I tried, but I didn't make it.

At that moment, I felt my necklace warm my heart a little. The small burst of energy re-ignited hope in me. I lifted my head to the side and looked back at Peacemaker. I felt he was sending me strength. Then I had a realization. I looked over my shoulder at the black horse.

"You can kill me. You can do whatever you like. But I am living right now where nothing is holding me back." As I lay there, I yelled, "I believe! I want this healing. I want a better life. I want to go to the next level. I want more. I know that all things are possible with God. I have not come this far to give up now!"

"Enough!" he yelled back into the lessening light of day. "Let's see you deal with this!" The black horse lifted up his front legs, gaining momentum to come down hard with intention to kill me with his two front feet.

As I sensed the weight of his feet leave my back, I felt an incredible amount of energy and power, which I used to spin to the left while yelling, "Arrrgh!" I managed to roll hard just out of the way as he stomped his feet down hard into the ground, committed to the intensity of his landing point. "You cannot hurt me. You cannot defeat me," I said with strength as I stood up.

"Really?" he sneered.

"Yes, really. You cannot do anything that I do not allow you to. I walked boldly toward my goal, finally realizing my inner power. He ran at me again. This time, something was different. I did not need to fight or engage or cower and protect myself. I just put out my hand, facing my fear with a courage and conviction. He could not penetrate my personal space, stopping just short of my hand.

He quickly moved around me to find a way to get to me. But it was like I had a force field surrounding me. I continued to walk safely and made it to the line of the woods just as the sun sunk behind the mountain.

"Yahoo!" I yelled with delight as the black horse let out a piercing whinny and galloped off into the distance, leaving a shadow and the dust behind him.

Peacemaker ran up to me. "Well done, my friend. You have completed the quest and defeated your fears."

I relished the moment. I had come face-to-face with my fear and I managed to conquer it. "I couldn't have done it without you."

Peacemaker lifted his head high. "I am so proud of where you have come from. You have learned so much and you are prepared to share it freely with others. That is a fantastic gift."

"Thank you," I replied. I really received his compliment deep in my heart. "It was quite an adventure," I sighed with satisfaction.

"What has been your biggest highlight?" he inquired.

"Finding out that my expectations of just being able to do things have been both a stumbling block and a huge asset. An obstacle because of the disappointment when it isn't perfect and doesn't happen quickly. An asset because it has given me the ability to go forward

blindly, trusting it will work out somehow. Gaining these dreams, smashing down my own huge obstacles, has taken time and effort, and the process has been the growing and making of me. So, I guess my words of wisdom and encouragement from this experience are, 'Keep going for the dream. Not only will you make it, but the growth and discoveries along the way may surprise, delight, and scare you'.

"I made it. Now that I have a taste of what that means, I can fully live it. I so appreciate this quest. It has made wonderful shifts in me. Yes, yes, yes!"

Where Nothing Holds Me Back

As I climbed aboard my friend and ally, I said, "It feels like my two worlds are moving closer and closer together," I explained. "My reality feels like a dream and my dreams are moving closer to reality."

"Very good. I like that," Peacemaker replied.

"Thank you Peacemaker for taking me on this quest. It has not only helped me to heal more, it has made me appreciate my life more. It has helped me to move to the next place. My heart feels freer to be open to let people see the authentic me. That is huge."

"You are most welcome. It was in you the entire time. I was just helping you to see it." He seemed to smile as he shook his whole body.

"Hey you!" I said, laughing with him.

"Hold on," Peacemaker said. We cantered through the woods again. I got down low, enjoying the speed, wind blowing through my hair. Peacemaker stopped.

"This looks familiar," I said, seeing where we started the journey. I slid down off his back and gave him a great big hug.

"We made it just in time," he said as he glanced at the last hues of the sun's light dipping beyond the horizon as

the full moon began to shine its silvery glow over the land.

"What do you mean?"

"Look at your necklace."

I pulled the necklace over my head and looked at it.

"Anything look different?" he asked. I held the necklace right in front of my face in the shaft of moonlight.

"No, it still has the same color with all the lines and cracks on the inside."

"Yes, just like your heart."

"Oh!" Then my necklace started its bright red glow, shining brighter than I had seen it before. Then my white inner light shined brightly back from within.

"Wow, what is happening?"

"You have completed your quest."

The two lights shined together. The necklace flew out of my hand and grew to the size of a basketball as it hovered five feet out and about eye level in front of me.

We watched it as many of the cracks started to disappear. It looked like the finger of a surgeon mending them back together. The necklace moved toward me, joining into my white light, and then moved directly in front of my heart.

The necklace pushed a force field of healing energy into my heart with a whoosh. I felt it penetrate to my very being, nearly knocking me off my feet with its intensity.

The powerful energy captivated me, giving me a tingling sensation throughout my entire body. I felt at peace with my life and my direction. I felt elated and restored.

Then the necklace shrunk back to size and popped into my hand, once again an inanimate object.

"Wow!" There were no more words to describe what I had just experienced. I was speechless.

Peacemaker smiled at me. "You can take that necklace, the glasses, and the brush back home to your world with you. They will be a reminder of the healing and the return to your heart. Stay in that place where nothing holds you back."

I looked in my knapsack at the gifts Peacemaker had given me, about to show him the broken glasses. But to my surprise, they were no longer broken. They had somehow fixed themselves.

"Come and visit again any time," he encouraged.

"Oh, I will," I replied with tears of thankfulness in my eyes, embracing this new feeling. "I am going to miss you."

"Remember, I am always with you." Peacemaker dropped his head against my side and gave me a nuzzle with his nose. Then he backed up and did a stunning rear, looking almost luminous in the moonlight. With a loud whinny he turned and galloped off.

"Goodbye Peacemaker," I said quietly to myself. I smiled seeing his exuberance and energy. Then to my surprise, I saw a bright shaft of light come out of the heavens, shining a few feet from Peacemaker. As he approached the beam of energy, his wings reappeared and he started to fly into the light, then into the clouds, with a shimmering white glow surrounding him.

My mouth was wide open as I watched, realizing that he is my Guardian Angel. The meaning of him saying he is always with me now made complete sense.

"Thank you," I sighed, and with this strong knowing in my heart, I felt overwhelmed with the full sense of being loved and looked after. "Thank you Peacemaker."

I happily turned with a big smile on my face and started running through the woods, excited to see my family and share my adventures with them.

A strange feeling of excited anticipation settled in my heart. Who knows where the next quest will take me?

About the Author

There was something that captivated Rachel about horses from early in her life, an indescribable attraction. Was it their looks or presence? She's not sure. But she did know she wanted to be around them from an early age. At twelve her dream was realized when she got her first horse. Her intuition was confirmed: A life with horses in it was the only way to go. However, understanding these gorgeous creatures was not as straightforward as she had imagined. Natural Horsemanship helped her with that.

Learning how to get a true connection with horses on a whole other level was a demanding and exhilarating journey. Her passion grew, and she knew she had to share the incredible connection she had discovered, becoming a horsemanship coach and instructor. She loves seeing people learn and excel with their horses. She also loves encouraging people to believe in themselves and let the horse take them on a wondrous journey of uncovering their dreams.

As an author driven to leave a legacy to her daughter, Rachel has combined her writing skills, horsemanship knowledge, and a dash of imagination to share her

journey of discovering how to live where nothing holds her back on the road to achieving all of her dreams.

Rachel's deepest desire is to bless her daughter, the horses, all people young at heart who are looking to reach their dreams, and especially the orphans who deserve to see their dreams with horses come true.

Rachel currently lives in Hamilton, Montana with her incredible husband Don and beautiful daughter, Shona Angelina.

She loves being a horsemanship instructor and coach, wife, mother, and author. But most important, she enjoys learning and heading toward new and stimulating growth as she fulfills more dreams by "Living where nothing holds her back."

Dreams with Horses

Join us at
DreamsWithHorses.com
Sign up for Free
Video and Updates

CPSIA information can be obtained at www.ICGtesting.com
Printed in the USA
BVOW071505220412

288295BV00001B/1/P